THE ARTS AND THE WORLD OF BUSINESS

second edition

by

CHARLOTTE GEORGI

The Scarecrow Press, Inc.

Metuchen, N.J. & London

1979

Library of Congress Cataloging in Publication Data

Georgi, Charlotte.
    The arts and the world of business.

    A rev. and updated bibliography, superseding all
previous versions.
    Includes index.
        1.   Arts--Management--Bibliography.   I.   Title.
Z5956.A7G46   1978   [NX760]   016.658'91'7
ISBN 0-8108-1174-X   78-12103

PREFACE

This bibliography is the result of some ten years of work in locating, acquiring, and processing the materials cited. Along the way, five bibliographies have been prepared. Two were published by the UCLA Study Center for Cultural Policy and Management in the Arts: The Arts and the Art of Administration (51 pages, 1970) and Management and the Arts (51 pages, 1972). These were coordinated and updated to produce the first edition of The Arts and the World of Business, published by the Scarecrow Press (123 pages, 1973). The Center has since published Supplement I (64 pages, 1974) and Supplement II (67 pages, 1976).

All five of these bibliographies have now been merged, updated, and revised to produce this second edition, which supersedes all previous publications. This comprehensive bibliography is arranged in sixteen subject and five form sections with an index by author and a section giving publishers' addresses.

All of these publications have been prepared in support of the courses designed for the master's degree program in the arts management field of concentration, first offered in the fall quarter of 1969 by the Graduate School of Management of the University of California Los Angeles.

With some few exceptions, all materials described are located in the UCLA libraries, chiefly in the Graduate School of Management Library. For the most part, the books included are recent imprints (1965 on) and are English-language, primarily American, publications.

Some explanatory remarks: Section XX cites several bibliographies which note older imprints and foreign materials. No specific journal and periodical articles are listed per se. Instead, Section XVII suggests various indexes which provide access to the enormous amount of such material available. Section XVIII lists selected basic journals, newsletters and newspapers.

My special thanks are due to Professor Hyman R. Faine, founder and director (1970-1974); Dr. Ichak Adizes, director (1975); Dr. Lee Cooper, director (1976-); and Ms. Barbara Capell, administrative assistant, of the Management in the Arts Program for their support, both moral and financial. I am particularly grateful to Professor Faine for his discerning foreword to the first edition and to Professor Cooper for his "secondword."

I wish to make very special mention of Marcelle Fortier, head of the UCLA Graduate School of Management Publications Services, a never-failing friend-in-need, always a source of both practical encouragement and moral support.

As with everything else in the Graduate School of Management Library, the staff have shown unflagging interest in these bibliographical ventures. I greatly appreciate their discovering and calling to my attention many of the titles cited. Mrs. Eloisa Gomez Yeargain and Mrs. Marlene Shaughnessy, my associate librarians, have been particularly helpful. Miss Marianne Roos, a student assistant of several years, now about to graduate from the UCLA Library School, did yeoman work as a bibliographical assistant in assembling the materials for the first rough draft.

To repeat the last paragraph of my Preface to the first edition of this work--which is as true today (maybe truer!) than when I first wrote it in 1972:

> And, finally, it is thanks to the diligent intelligence as well as the clerical skill of Mrs. Terry Fate that everything was ever assembled to the actual point of typing the final draft copy.

Charlotte Georgi
Graduate School of Management Library
University of California Los Angeles
March 1978

TABLE OF CONTENTS

52526

FOREWORD TO SECOND EDITION

The publication of the second edition of The Arts and the World of Business is a measure of the growth of an emerging field and the permanence of interest on the part of professional arts managers in improving their ability to approach and seek solutions for the enormously complex problems facing the arts.

A primary role for this bibliography is communication. Traditional organization in the arts has gone along disciplinary lines. Much of the management of museums has evolved from art and art history study. The study of organization in symphony orchestras was not required reading. Yet museums have much to learn from the trials and triumphs of symphony orchestras as well as much that they could teach. While the forms have had unique artistic evolutions, they share many problems in common in the struggle for survival as creative entities.

The union of art and business represents an edge which cuts across disciplinary boundaries. Arts management provides a common language so that those whose love is dance can learn from the collective efforts of the people devoted to the advancement of theater. There need be no zero-sum competition among various arts disciplines. Communication across boundaries is a prerequisite for the understanding of shared challenges and opportunities.

If we look to the near future of arts management, we can see that university faculties are drawing toward investigating the issues facing artists and arts organizations. They are willing to use their skills to further the arts world. This means the evolution of theory to facilitate professional practice. The role of theory is the systematic accumulation of knowledge. This bibliography fosters the evolution of theory by collecting and organizing the existing writings in a way useful to scholars, students of arts management, and professionals working for the betterment of the arts.

In sum, Charlotte Georgi has created a companion
for those involved in the advancement of study in that most
delicate of bonds, the relation between art and the organizations which sustain art. On behalf of a program dedicated
to the study and practice of arts management, I thank her.

LEE G. COOPER
Associate Professor and
Management in the Arts Program Director

Graduate School of Management
University of California Los Angeles
January 1978

FOREWORD TO FIRST EDITION

For some time there has been a growing recognition in both the performing and visual arts fields of the need for training arts administrator-managers in the arts.

The words "arts management" strike consternation, confusion and sometimes antagonism in the minds of some people when they are first heard. Images of a "manager" of an artist, resembling a "fight" manager or the manager of an actor or singer, flash by; sometimes the feeling of a contradiction in terms is engendered. How can an art which has its origin in creativity, the unexpected, the imagined, the unknown, be managed? It is as if one were to harness the heat and light of a lightning bolt. At other times the image is one of manipulation, of control of the arts, or of ends justifying the means.

These difficulties of joining the words "arts" and "management" to describe the activity of a specific human being become even more pronounced when they are used to describe a course of study, of training, of research and analysis. These were some of the basic puzzlements confronting those of us involved in the discussions in 1969 when we first met on the West and East coasts to consider the need, the applicability and the possibility of establishing in the UCLA Graduate School of Business Administration (as it was then known) a center of training for arts administrators.

Participating in these discussions were faculty members of the Business School and the departments of Art, Dance, Music and Theater Arts of the UCLA College of Fine Arts, as well as practitioners, directors, executives of many of the arts institutions and organizations in the United States, and representatives of state and federal agencies involved in the arts. It was a highly knowledgeable, volatile, opinionated and vocal group.

The consensus that was reached among us was that

ix

there was definitely a need for training the future managers of arts institutions. Such training could best be achieved in a School of Management in cooperation with a College of Fine Arts where all the art disciplines and facilities were represented and available. It was further felt that the arts institutions in the Los Angeles area should have a close, direct and interdependent relationship with the training and educational process.

As a participant in the discussions on the East Coast, I felt, as many others did, that the existing methods of developing arts managers were inadequate to the present and future needs of the arts. This was true whether advancement was by working one's way up from "coffee getter," or by lateral movements from other fields such as law, accounting, fund raising or advertising, or even by being an "artist" first and becoming a manager when one had reached the end of his career as an artist.

Many of us felt that what the arts organizations needed were executives with skills in management equally as broad and developed as those possessed by managers of other types of human enterprises; that fundamentally a museum or a theater was an organization conceived by human beings, managed by human beings to achieve an objective of worth and need for human beings. In essence this met the definition of a manufacturing, distributive or service organization, and schools of management in the U.S. had been training individuals to do this very thing for many years with considerable success. Such schools and their faculties had been doing research, analyzing and developing theories, methods, approaches and concepts to make such organizations function effectively for the purposes for which they were organized.

Then, as now, I felt that these methods could be applied successfully to arts institutions, for the benefit of the institutions, the creative artists, and the public which they served. There are, however, some fundamental differences between an automobile company and a symphony orchestra, between the manufacture of an automobile and the presentation of a symphony. These are crucial to the management of the organization and, of course, to the training of the manager.

For one, the auto manufacturer sells his car to make a profit for the owners of his company, while the director of the orchestra neither expects nor reaps any profits. In fact he knows that his orchestra's activities will generate a deficit.

In other words he is, and would be, managing a "not for profit" organization.

For another, the arts institution has an obligation to the past, as well as to the present, to the preservation of classic art as well as the exhibition and presentation of the modern, and, as we are learning, to the encouragement of the innovator and the future creator who will supplant and supplement the classicist and the modernist.

As we at UCLA began to develop the academic program, the curriculum, the teaching methods and materials necessary for the training of our students, several things became clearly apparent. Our students would have to gain knowledge in statistics, accounting, economics, systems analysis, organizational behavior, marketing, model building, computer operations and managerial decision-making. These subjects were all being taught within the School of Management. There were teachers, reading materials, syllabi, texts, cases, films and many other sources of information and knowledge for them.

However, for the arts manager there were many other areas which would have to be taught and in which the students would have to become proficient, to learn the issues and problems, to search for some of the answers and to begin to develop the skills and knowledge uniquely essential to managing arts organizations. These were so varied, so intertwined and interrelated, and they covered such a wide spectrum of human activities that just to list them became a problem.

The student would have to know the economics of a not-for-profit organization; the legal problems involved in organizing, conducting and supporting such an entity; the special industrial and labor relations issues and elements in an art organization; the relationship of art to society, to social issues, to minority groups, to the particular community in which it is located; as well as the special role which government at all levels can and does have with artistic bodies. In short, we would have to teach law, labor relations, sociology, government, public administration, taxation, aesthetics, and even the politics and history of our country and its multifaceted society.

This was a tall order for the faculty of the Management School to meet, even though we had the participation of faculty members of the College of Fine Arts and the School of Law at UCLA. There were few, if any, people trained to teach these subjects within the context of arts management. Gradually such a group has developed and is beginning to meet the needs of a growing number of students training to become arts managers.

However, there was another equally serious problem. This was the relative absence of textbooks, research material, readings, data, statistics, analytical documentation, theoretical formulations and the like. This was not only true in the specifics of each of the areas just mentioned, but also in the interrelationship of each of the areas to the other--a very crucial element in the development of curricula and the teaching of students.

We in our Management in the Arts Program were thus extremely fortunate in having Charlotte Georgi as the chief librarian of the Graduate School of Management Library. From the very beginning Miss Georgi devoted her talents and knowledge to helping us solve this fundamental need of our program. Some preliminary work on our part indicated the tremendous task which we faced in seeking out what was already published, what was buried within past publications, in newspapers, magazines, trade journals, government and private reports. Miss Georgi combed the existing bibliographies, which were few in number, to see what was still relevant, obtainable or available. We cooperated on the task of getting reading lists of seminars, workshops, conferences, and of some widely scattered courses given in varied institutions and schools, though these were generally limited to but one area such as museums or symphony orchestras, whereas our program was training managers for dance companies, regional theater groups, arts councils and similar organizations which therefore required that the student learn the principles and techniques applicable to all these fields rather than one.

This was a formidable task. It was compounded by the myriad of arts organizations flourishing in the U.S. and the fact that arts councils at the federal, state, county and municipal levels were springing up as quickly as fresh grass after a heavy rainfall.

What Charlotte Georgi has done is to help the process of analysis of the components of the field of arts management. Her bibliography is analogous to the cartography of an un-

charted and newly discovered land. It is a guide to the prac-
titioner, the lawyer, the administrator, the accountant, a
member of the board of directors, a trustee of a foundation,
a government official, a corporation executive, a layman in
the arts, and the citizen interested in the quality of life and
art in the U.S. It enables these persons and many others
to begin to see the role and function of art and arts institutions in our society, to learn the beginnings, the present
problems and the directions of future trends. Charlotte
Georgi's work thus is an education in itself for those seeking
guidance and information; it directs them to what is available
in print today and what yet remains to be written, thought
about and researched in the future. The knowledge contained
in this volume and obtained by reading the reference material
will, I am sure, become the beginning of wisdom for the
many who will read it, learn from it and use it as a foundation and guide to future knowledge.

For this, and for her helpfulness, guidance and pa-
tience, I am deeply grateful, as are all of us involved in the
Arts Management Program at UCLA. We now are aware of
what is available to us. We and the others who will follow
us, whether teachers, students, researchers or concerned
citizens, can now begin the task of supplementing and adding
to Charlotte Georgi's work.

HYMAN R. FAINE
Professor,
Management in the Arts Program

Graduate School of Management
University of California Los Angeles

I

BUSINESS, ECONOMICS, AND THE ARTS

Adizes, Ichak. "Administering for the Arts--Problems in Practice." Los Angeles: Graduate School of Management, University of California, 1971. 26p. (Management in the Arts Research Paper no. 15.)

Adizes, Ichak. "UCLA Conferences on Arts Administration: Summary of the Meetings and a Report on Implementation." Los Angeles: Graduate School of Management, University of California, 1969. 34p. (Management in the Arts Research Paper no. 1.)

Adizes, Ichak. "The Unique Character of Performing Arts Organizations and the Functioning of Their Boards of Directors (A Managerial Analysis)." Los Angeles: Graduate School of Management, University of California, 1971. 14p. (Management in the Arts Research Paper no. 4.)

Adler, Richard, and Walter S. Baer, editors. The Electronic Box Office: Humanities and Arts on the Cable. New York: Praeger, 1974. 139p.

Anderson, Robert O. "The Arts--Challenge to Business. Excerpts from an address to the Seattle, Washington, Chamber of Commerce on April 14, 1970." New York: Business Committee for the Arts, 1970. 15p.

The Art Investment Report. Fortnightly. Wall Street Reports Pub. Co. 120 Wall Street, New York, N.Y. 10005.

Artist and Advocate: An Essay on Corporate Patronage. Edited by Nina Kaiden and Bartlett Hayes. New York: Renaissance Editions, 1967. 93p.

Artist's Market '76. Edited by Kirk Polking and Liz Prince. Cincinnati: Writer's Digest, 1975. 624p.

1

Arts Council of Great Britain. Training Arts Administrators. Report of the Committee on Enquiry into Arts Administration Training. London: Arts Council of Great Britain, 1971. 76p.

Bell, Daniel. The Cultural Contradictions of Capitalism. New York: Basic Books, 1976. 301p.

Berlye, Milton K. Selling Your Art Work: A Marketing Guide for Fine & Commercial Artists. South Brunswick, N.J.: A. S. Barnes, 1973. 272p.

Blodgett, Richard E. How to Make Money in the Art Market. New York: Peter H. Wyden, 1975. 267p.

Business Committee for the Arts. Business in the Arts Awards: A Ten-Year History, 1966-75. New York, 1975. 88p.

Business Committee for the Arts. "1426 Examples of How BCA Companies Supported the Arts in '74 & '75." New York, 1975. 31p.

Business Committee for the Arts. "1776 and More Examples of How BCA Companies Supported the Arts in 1975 and 1976." New York, 1976. 35p.

Business Committee for the Arts. "2,507 Examples of How BCA Companies Supported the Arts in '76 and '77." New York, 1977. 35p.

Business in the Arts '70. Gideon Chagy, editor. New York: Paul S. Eriksson, 1970. 176p.

Center Theatre Group. Box Office Guidelines. New York: Foundation for the Extension and Development of the American Professional Theatre, 1974. 44p.

Chamberlain, Betty. The Artist's Guide to His Market. 2d ed. New York: Watson-Guptill, 1975. 176p.

Churchill, Allen. The Splendor Seekers: An Informal Glimpse of America's Multimillionaire Spenders--Members of the $50,000,000 Club. New York: Grosset & Dunlap, 1974. 278p.

Connaughton, Howard W. Craftsmen in Business: A Guide

to Financial Management and Taxes. New York: American Crafts Council, 1975. 73p.

Contemporary Crafts Market Place. Irregular. Compiled by
the American Crafts Council, Ann Arbor, Mich.:
Bowker.

Costa, Sylvia Allen. How to Prepare a Production Budget
for Film & Video Tape. 2d ed. Blue Ridge Summit,
Pa.: Tab Books, 1975. 192p.

The Crafts Report. Monthly newsletter. Crafts Report Pub.
Co., Brooklyn, N.Y. 11230.

Dawson, William M. A Residency Handbook. Madison,
Wis.: Association of College, University and Community Arts Administrators, Inc., 1975. 46p.

Diamant, Lincoln, editor. The Anatomy of a Television
Commercial. New York: Hastings House, 1970. 191p.

Educational Facilities Laboratories. "Technical Assistance
for Arts Facilities." New York: Educational Facilities
Laboratories, 1977. 32p.

Eells, Richard Sedric Fox. The Corporation and the Arts.
New York: Macmillan, 1967. 365p.

Fine Arts Market Place. Biennial. Edited by Paul Cummings. R. R. Bowker Co., New York.

Ford Foundation. Finances of the Performing Arts. Volume
I, A Survey of 166 Professional Nonprofit Resident
Theaters, Operas, Symphonies, Ballets, and Modern
Dance Companies. Volume II, A Survey of the Char-
acters and Attitudes of Audiences for Theater, Opera,
Symphony, and Ballet in 12 U.S. Cities. New York,
1974. 2 volumes.

Foundation for the Extension and Development of the American Professional Theatre. Subscription Guidelines.
New York, 1975. Various pagings.

Galbraith, John Kenneth. The Liberal Hour. Boston:
Houghton Mifflin, 1960. 197p. See Essay III, "Economics and Art."

Galbraith, John Kenneth. The New Industrial State. 2d ed.,
    rev. Boston: Houghton Mifflin, 1971. 423p.

Gingrich, Arnold. Business & the Arts: An Answer to To-
    morrow. Foreword by David Rockefeller. New York:
    Paul Eriksson, 1969. 141p.

Gladstone, M. J. A Report on Professional Salaries in New
    York State Museums. New York: New York State As-
    sociation of Museums, 1972. 47p.

Goodman, Calvin J., with Florence J. Goodman. Marketing
    Art: A Handbook for Artists and Art Dealers. Los
    Angeles: Gee Tee Bee, 1972. 318p.

Heery, George T. Time, Cost and Architecture. New York:
    McGraw-Hill, 1975. 212p.

Henle, Guenter. Three Spheres: A Life in Politics, Business
    and Music: The Autobiography of Guenter Henle. Chi-
    cago: Henry Regnery, 1971. 277p.

Henry, Austin H., and E. Arthur Prieve. Improved Financial
    Management of Smaller Performing Arts Organizations.
    Madison: Center for Arts Administration, Graduate
    School of Business, University of Wisconsin, 1973.

Hilkert, Robert N. A Humanist's View: "The Arts of Man-
    agement" and Other Talks. Philadelphia: Federal Re-
    serve Bank of Philadelphia, 1970. 46p.

Holcomb, Bill. Fear of Filing: A Beginner's Handbook for
    Dancers and Other Artists on Record Keeping and Fed-
    eral Taxes. New York: Volunteer Lawyers for the
    Arts, 1975. 39p.

Kaderlan, Norman S. The Role of the Arts Administrator.
    Madison: Center for Arts Administration, Graduate
    School of Business, University of Wisconsin, 1973. 47p.

Kintner, Earl Wilson, and Jack L. Lahr. An Intellectual
    Property Law Primer; A Survey of the Law of Patents,
    Trade Secrets, Trademarks, Franchises, Copyrights,
    and Personality and Entertainment Rights. New York:
    Macmillan, 1975. 539p.

Kort, Michele F. White-Collar Unions in Art Museums: The

Collective Response. Comprehensive research paper for UCLA Management in the Arts Program. Los Angeles: University of California Los Angeles Graduate School of Management, 1974. 85p.

Kotler, Philip. Marketing for Nonprofit Organizations. Englewood Cliffs, N. J. : Prentice-Hall, 1975. 436p.

Krawitz, Herman E. , with Howard K. Klein. Royal American Symphonic Theater: A Radical Proposal for a Subsidized Professional Theater. New York: Macmillan, 1975. 211p.

Lee, James C. Do or Die; Survival for Nonprofits. Washington, D. C. : Taft Products, 1974. 102p.

Legal and Business Problems of the Motion Picture Industry. Paul A. Baumgarten, chairman. New York: Practising Law Institute, 1973. 616p.

Lidstone, Herrick K. Exempt Organizations and the Arts. New York: Volunteer Lawyers for the Arts, 1975. Various pagings.

Lidstone, Herrick K. The Individual Artist: Recordkeeping, Methods of Accounting, Income and Itemized Deductions for Federal Income Tax Purposes. New York: Volunteer Lawyers for the Arts, 1976. 52p.

Management Science Applications to Leisure-Time Operations. Edited by Shaul P. Ladany. New York: American Elsevier, 1975. 373p.

Mayer, Michael F. The Film Industries: Practical Business/Legal Problems in Production, Distribution, and Exhibition. New York: Hastings House, 1973. 212p.

Middlemas, Robert Keith. The Double Market: Art Theft and Art Thieves. Farnborough, England: Saxon House, 1975. 237p.

National Council of YMCA's. Training Volunteer Leaders. Fairfax, Va. : NTL Learning Resources Corp. , 1974. 189p.

Nelson, Charles A. , and Frederick J. Turk. Financial Management for the Arts: A Guidebook for Arts Organizations. New York: Associated Councils of the Arts, 1975. 52p.

Noll, Roger G.; Merton J. Peck, and John J. McGowan. Economic Aspects of Television Regulation. Washington, D. C.: Brookings Institution, 1973. 342p.

Oleck, Howard L. Non-Profit Corporations, Organizations, and Associations. 3d ed. Englewood Cliffs, N. J.: Prentice-Hall, 1974. 1000p.

Osborne, Alfred E. "On Analyzing the Economics of the Non-Profit Theatre." Paper presented at meeting of the University of California Los Angeles, Graduate School of Management, Management in the Arts Study Center, May 18, 1977. 7p.

Pfeffer, Irving. "Fine Arts: A Program in Risk Management." Los Angeles: Graduate School of Management, University of California, 1971. 34p. (Management in the Arts Research Paper no. 7.)

Phillips, Gene D. The Movie Makers: Artists in an Industry. Chicago: Nelson-Hall, 1973. 249p.

Photography Market Place. 2d ed. Edited by Fred W. McDarrah. Ann Arbor, Mich.: Bowker, 1977. 475p.

Poggi, Jack. Theater in America: The Impact of Economic Forces, 1870-1967. Ithaca, N. Y.: Cornell University Press, 1968. 328p.

Powers, Ron. The Newscasters: The News Business as Show Business. New York: St. Martin's Press, 1977. 243p.

Prieve, E. Arthur, and Ira W. Allen. Administration in the Arts: An Annotated Bibliography of Selected References. Madison: Center for Arts Administration, Graduate School of Business, University of Wisconsin, 1973. 111p.

Private Foundations and Business Corporations Active in Arts/ Humanities/Education. By Daniel Millsaps and editors of the Washington International Arts Letter. Washington, D. C.: Washington International Arts Letter, v. 1 1970, 138p.; v. 2 1974, 264p.

Quaal, Ward L., and James A. Brown. Broadcast Management: Radio and Television. 2d ed. New York: Hastings House, 1976. 464p.

Raymond, Thomas C.; Stephen A. Greyser, and Douglas
Schwalbe. Cases in Arts Administration. Rev. ed.
Cambridge, Mass.: Arts Administration Research In-
stitute, 1975. 389p.

Reichardt, Jasia. Cybernetic Serendipity: The Computer and
the Arts. New York: Praeger, 1969, 101p. Special
issue, August 1968, Studio International.

Reichardt, Jasia, compiler. Cybernetics, Art and Ideas.
Greenwich, Conn.: New York Graphic Society, 1971.
207p.

Reiss, Alvin H. The Arts Management Handbook: A Guide
for Those Interested in or Involved with the Administration of Cultural Institutions. 2d ed. With a preface by
Nancy Hanks. New York: Law-Arts Publishers, 1974.
802p.

Rodewald, Fred C., and Edward Gottschall. Commercial Art
as a Business. 2d rev. ed. New York: Viking, 1971.
173p.

Russell-Cobb, Trevor. Paying the Piper: The Theory and
Practice of Industrial Patronage. London: Queen Anne
Press, 1968. 111p.

Salem, Mahmoud. Organizational Survival in the Performing
Arts: The Making of the Seattle Opera. New York:
Praeger, 1976. 210p.

Schindler-Rainman, Eva, and Ronald Lippitt. Team Training
for Community Change: Concepts, Goals, Strategies &
Skills. Fairfax, Va.: NTL Learning Resources Corporation, 1972. 75p.

Scott, Michael. The Crafts Business Encyclopedia: Marketing,
Management, and Money. New York: Harcourt Brace
Jovanovich, 1977. 286p.

Seiden, Martin H. Who Controls the Mass Media? Popular
Myths and Economic Realities. New York: Basic
Books, 1974. 246p.

Seltzer, George. The Professional Symphony Orchestra in
the United States. Metuchen, N.J.: Scarecrow Press,
1975. 486p.

Shemel, Sidney, and M. William Krasilovsky. This Business of Music. Rev. & enl. ed. Edited by Paul Ackerman. New York: Billboard, 1977. 575p.

Smith, George Alan. Arts Administrator Need and Potential in New York State: A Study for the New York State Council on the Arts. Albany, N. Y. , 1968. 40p.

Spiro, Herbert T. Finance for the Nonfinancial Manager. New York: Wiley, 1977. 255p.

The State of the Arts and Corporate Support. Gideon Chagy, editor. New York: Paul S. Eriksson, 1971. 184p.

Statistical Research, Inc. A Study of the Consistency of Lo-cal Market Television Ratings. Westfield, N. J. , 1970.

Strauss, Victor. Graphic Arts Management. Philadelphia: Presentation Press, 1973. 340p.

A Survey of Arts Administration Training in the United States and Canada. New York: American Council of the Arts for the Center for Arts Administration, Graduate School of Business, University of Wisconsin-Madison, 1977. 69p. Rev. ed. of A Survey of Arts Administration Training in the United States and Canada, by Penny Fin-kelman and the Donner Foundation, 1975.

Taubman, Joseph. Performing Arts: Management and Law. New York: Law-Arts Publishers, 1974. (Supplement to the 1973 four-volume set.)

Tax Impacts on Philanthropy. By Douglas Dillon and others. Symposium conducted by the Tax Institute of America, Dec. 2-3, 1971, Washington, D. C. Princeton, N. J. : Tax Institute of America, 1972. 234p.

Theatre Communications Group. TCG Fiscal Survey. Annual. Prepared by James Copeland, program director. New York.

U. S. Library of Congress. Education and Public Welfare Division. Millions for the Arts: Federal and State Cul-tural Programs; An Exhaustive Senate Report. Wash-ington, D. C. : Washington International Arts Letter, 1972. 58p.

Video Resources in New York State. Prepared by the Film and Video Bureau with support from the New York State Council on the Arts. New York: Publishing Center for Cultural Resources, 1975. 64p.

Voegeli, Thomas J. Handbook for Tour Management. Madison: Center for Arts Administration, Graduate School of Business, University of Wisconsin, 1975. 55p.

Vogt, Marie. The Businessman's Ballet Book. Sylvania, Ohio, 1973. 50p.

The Volunteer Urban Consulting Group. Recruiting Business Executives for the Boards of Directors on Nonprofit Organizations. New York: Volunteer Urban Consulting Group, 1977. 52p.

Wainwright, Charles Anthony. Television Commercials: How to Create Successful TV Advertising. Rev. ed. New York: Hastings House, 1970. 318p.

Wayne, June. "The Selling of Art." Los Angeles: Tamarind Lithography Workshop, 1966. 12p.

Webber, Ross A. Culture and Management: Text and Readings in Comparative Management. Homewood, Ill. : Irwin, 1969. 598p.

Wehle, Mary M. Financial Management for Arts Organizations. Cambridge, Mass. : Arts Administration Research Institute, 1975. 163p.

II

CULTURE, LEISURE, AND THE ARTS

American Council for the Arts and Education. Panel on Arts, Education and America. Coming to Our Senses: The Significance of the Arts for American Education; A Panel Report. New York: McGraw-Hill, 1977. 334p.

Art and Sexual Politics: Women's Liberation, Women Artists, and Art History. Edited by Thomas B. Hess and Elizabeth C. Baker. New York: Macmillan, 1973. 150p.

Arts in Society. Ceased publication with v. 13, no. 2, Summer-Fall 1976; formerly 3 issues per year. Edward L. Kamarck, editor. University of Wisconsin-Extension. Book reviews, advertising, illustrations, index. Circulation was 5000. The following numbers are recommended:

Arts in the Community, v. 1, no. 5, Fall 1960.
California Institute of the Arts: Prologue to a Community, v. 7, no. 3, Fall-Winter 1970.
Confrontation Between Art and Technology, v. 6, no. 2, Summer-Fall 1969.
Education and the Arts, v. 2, no. 3, Spring-Summer 1963.
Environment and Culture, v. 9, no. 1, Spring-Summer 1972.
The Geography and Psychology of Urban Cultural Centers, v. 4, no. 3, Fall-Winter 1967.
The University as Cultural Leader in Society, v. 3, no. 4, Spring-Summer 1966.

The Arts on Campus: The Necessity for Change. By James Ackerman et al. Edited by Margaret Mahoney with the assistance of Isabel Moore. Greenwich, Conn.: New York Graphic Society, 1970. 143p.

Associated Councils of the Arts. A Guide to Community Arts Agencies. Edited by Michael K. Newton and Barbara B. Israel. New York, 1974. 373p.

Balio, Tino. United Artists: The Company Built by the Stars. Madison: University of Wisconsin Press, 1976. 323p.

Baynes, Ken. Art in Society. Woodstock, N. Y.: The Overlook Press, 1975. 288p.

Burnham, Bonnie. The Art Crisis. New York: St. Martin's Press, 1975. 256p.

Burns, Joan Simpson. The Awkward Embrace: The Creative Artist and the Institution in America. New York: Knopf, 1975. 512p.

Canadian Conference of the Arts. Direction Canada: A Declaration of Canadian Cultural Concern. Toronto, 1973. 78p.

Canfield, Cass. The Incredible Pierpont Morgan: Financier and Art Collector. New York: Harper & Row, 1974.

Carter on the Arts. New York: Associated Councils of the Arts, 1977. 74p.

Chagy, Gideon. The New Patrons of the Arts. New York: Harry N. Abrams, 1973. 128p.

Charlesworth, James Clyde, editor. Leisure in America: Blessing or Curse? Philadelphia: American Academy of Political and Social Science, 1964. 96p.

Churchill, Allen. The Splendor Seekers: An Informal Glimpse of America's Multimillionaire Spenders--Members of the $50,000,000 Club. New York: Grosset & Dunlap, 1974. 278p.

Clapp, Jane. Art Censorship: A Chronology of Proscribed and Prescribed Art. Metuchen, N. J.: Scarecrow Press, 1972. 582p.

Cultural Directory: Guide to Federal Funds and Services for Cultural Activities. Research conducted by Linda Coe. New York: Associated Councils of the Arts, 1975. 356p. (Originally published in 1971 under title, Washington and the Arts.)

Cultural Management Seminar, Boston, 1975. "Summary of the
  Cultural Management Seminar, February 13 and 14,
  1975. " Conducted for members of the Metropolitan Cul-
  tural Alliance by the Faculty of the Sloan School of
  Management, Massachusetts Institute of Technology.
  Edited by Susan Byers. Boston: Metropolitan Cultural
  Alliance, 1975. 28p.

Cultural Post. Irregularly published, 1-2 issues per year.
  National Endowment for the Arts, Washington, D. C.
  20506. Bibliographies, illustrations. Tabloid format.

Davis, Douglas M. Art and the Future; A History/Prophecy
  of the Collaboration Between Science, Technology, and
  Art. New York: Praeger, 1973. 208p.

Dumazedier, Joffre. Toward a Society of Leisure, translated
  from the French by Stewart E. McClure. New York:
  Free Press, 1967. 307p.

Eames, John Douglas. The MGM Story: The Complete History of Fifty Roaring Years. New York: Crown, 1975.
  400p.

Easton, Carol. The Search for Sam Goldwyn. New York:
  Morrow, 1976. 304p.

Gans, Herbert J. Popular Culture and High Culture. New
  York: Basic Books, 1974. 179p.

Getting the Message Across: An Inquiry Into Successes and
  Failures of Cross-Cultural Communication in the Contemporary World. New York: Unesco, 1975. 214p.

Girard, Augustin. Cultural Development: Experiences and
  Policies. Paris: Unesco, 1972. 145p.

Greenfield, Jeff. Television: The First Fifty Years. New
  York: Abrams, 1977. 280p.

Hall, James B. , and Barry Ulanov. Modern Culture and the
  Arts. 2d ed. New York: McGraw-Hill, 1972. 574p.

Hart, Philip. Orpheus in the New World: The Symphony
  Orchestra as an American Cultural Institution. New
  York: Norton, 1973. 562p.

Harvard Summer School Institute in Arts Administration. Cultural Policy and Arts Administration. Edited by Stephen A. Greyser. Cambridge, Mass.; distributed by Harvard University Press, 1973. 173p.

Heery, George T. Time, Cost, and Architecture. New York: McGraw-Hill, 1975. 212p.

Hess, John L. The Grand Acquisitors. Boston: Houghton Mifflin, 1974. 160p.

Higham, Charles. Warner Brothers. New York: Scribner's 1975. 232p.

Johnson, Alton C., and E. Arthur Prieve. Older Americans: The Unrealized Audience for the Arts. Madison: Center for Arts Administration, Graduate School of Business, University of Wisconsin, 1976. 51p.

Johnson, Priscilla. Khrushchev and the Arts: The Politics of Soviet Culture, 1962-1964. Cambridge, Mass.: MIT Press, 1965. 300p.

Jowett, Garth. Film: The Democratic Art. Boston: Little, Brown, 1976. 518p.

Kranzberg, Melvin, and William H. Davenport. Technology and Culture; An Anthology. New York: Schocken Books, 1972. 364p.

Levine, Faye. The Culture Barons. New York: T. Y. Crowell, 1976. 312p.

Linder, Steffan B. The Harried Leisure Class. New York: Columbia University Press, 1970. 182p.

McLuhan, Herbert Marshall. Culture Is Our Business. New York: McGraw-Hill, 1970. 336p.

McMullen, Roy. Art, Affluence, and Alienation; The Fine Arts Today. New York: Praeger, 1968. 272p.

Management Science Applications to Leisure-Time Operations. Edited by Shaul P. Ladany. New York: American Elsevier, 1975. 373p.

Mark, Charles C. A Study of Cultural Policy in the United

States. Paris: United Nations Educational, Scientific and Cultural Organization, 1969. 43p. (Studies and Documents on Cultural Policies no. 2.)

Miller, Lillian B. Patrons and Patriotism; The Encouragement of the Fine Arts in the United States, 1790-1860. Chicago: University of Chicago Press, 1966. 335p.

Minihan, Janet. The Nationalization of Culture: The Development of State Subsidies to the Arts in Great Britain. New York: New York University Press, 1977. 276p.

Morrison, Jack. The Rise of the Arts on the American Campus. New York: McGraw-Hill, 1973. 223p.

National Committee for Cultural Resources. "National Report on the Arts." New York, 1975. 36p.

National Endowment for the Arts. Creative America: Arts & The Pursuit of Happiness. Washington, D. C.: U. S. Government Printing Office, 1976. 32p.

National Endowment for the Arts. New Dimensions for the Arts, 1971-1972. Washington, D. C.: U. S. Government Printing Office, 1973.

National Research Center of the Arts. "Americans and the Arts: Highlights." New York: Associated Councils of the Arts, 1974. 36p.

National Research Center of the Arts. Americans and the Arts: A Survey of Public Opinion. New York: Associated Councils of the Arts, 1975. 162p.

National Research Center of the Arts. Californians and the Arts. Sacramento: California Arts Commission, n. d.

National Research Center of the Arts. A Study of the Non-Profit Arts and Cultural Industry of New York State. New York, 1972. 194p.

New Deal Art Projects; An Anthology of Memoirs. Edited by Francis V. O'Connor. Washington, D. C.: Smithsonian Institution, 1972. 339p.

New York (City). Mayor's Committee on Cultural Policy.

Report of the Mayor's Committee on Cultural Policy,
    October 15, 1974. New York, 1974. 87p.

New York (State). Commission on Cultural Resources. Arts
    and the Schools: Patterns for Better Education; Report.
    Albany, 1972. 100p.

New York (State). Commission on Cultural Resources. Cul-
    tural Resource Development. New York: Praeger,
    1976. 219p.

Newton, Michael, and Scott Hatley. Persuade and Provide;
    The Story of the Arts and Education Council in St.
    Louis. With an introduction by Nancy Hanks. New
    York: Associated Councils of the Arts, 1970. 249p.

On the Future of Art. By Arnold J. Toynbee et al. Intro-
    duction by Edward F. Fry. New York: Viking, 1970.
    134p.

Owen, John D. The Price of Leisure: An Economic Analysis
    of the Demand for Leisure Time. Rotterdam: Rotter-
    dam University Press, 1969. 169p.

Parker, Stanley. The Future of Work and Leisure. New
    York: Praeger, 1971. 160p.

Pasquill, Frank T. , and Joan Horsman. Wooden Pennies:
    A Report on Cultural Funding Patterns in Canada. Tor-
    onto: York University, Programme in Arts Administra-
    tion, 1973. 75p.

Reiss, Alvin H. Culture and Company: A Critical Study of
    an Improbable Alliance. New York: Twayne, 1972.
    309p.

Schindler-Rainman, Eva, and Ronald Lippitt. Team Training
    for Community Change: Concepts, Goals, Strategies &
    Skills. Fairfax, Va. : NTL Learning Resources Corp. ,
    1972. 75p.

Schwalbe, Douglas, and Janet Baker-Carr. Conflict in the
    Arts: The Relocation of Authority. Volume 1, The
    Arts Council. Volume 2, The Orchestra. Volume 3,
    The Museum. Cambridge, Mass. : Arts Administration
    Research Institute, 1976-1977. Various pagings.

Simon, Yves René Marie. Work, Society, and Culture. Edited by Vukan Kuie. Bronx, N. Y. : Fordham University Press, 1971. 234p.

The Sociology of the Arts. Edited by Mildred Weil and Duncan Hartley. Danville, Ill. : Interstate Printers & Publishers, 1975. 179p.

Spradley, James P. , and Michael A. Rynkiewich. The Nacirema: Readings on American Culture. Boston: Little, Brown, 1975. 417p.

Tax Impacts on Philanthropy. By Douglas Dillon and others. Symposium conducted by the Tax Institute of America, Dec. 2-3, 1971, Washington, D. C. Princeton, N. J. : Tax Institute of America, 1972. 234p.

Technology and Culture: An Anthology. Edited by Melvin Kranzberg and William H. Davenport. New York: Schocken, 1972. 364p.

Technology, Human Values, and Leisure. Edited by Max Kaplan and Phillip Bosserman. Nashville, Tenn. : Abingdon Press, 1971. 256p.

Veblen, Thorstein. The Theory of the Leisure Class. Introduction by Robert Lekachman. New York: Viking, 1967. 400p.

Webber, Ross A. , compiler. Culture and Management; Text and Readings in Comparative Management. Homewood, Ill. : Richard D. Irwin, 1969. 598p.

III

FOUNDATIONS, GRANTS AND FUND-RAISING

About Foundations: How to Find the Facts You Need to Get
a Grant. Rev. ed. by Judith B. Margolin. New York:
The Foundation Center, 1977. 48p.

Abrahams, Peter D. The Bread Game: The Realities of
Foundation Fundraising. San Francisco: Glide Publications, 1974. 96p.

Accounting Advisory Committee. "Report to the Commission
on Private Philanthropy and Public Needs. " Washington,
D. C. : Price Waterhouse, 1974. 36p.

Advisory Committee on Endowment Management. Managing
Educational Endowments; Report to the Ford Foundation.
New York: Ford Foundation, 1969. 65p.

The Anatomy of an Art Auction; A Vital Guide for Organization Fund Raisers. Commack, N. Y. : Arnold Harvey
Associates, 1972. 77p.

Andrews, Frank Emerson. Foundation Watcher. Lancaster,
Pa. : Franklin and Marshall College, 1973. 321p.

Annual Register of Grant Support. Los Angeles: Academic
Media.

Ayer Public Relations and Publicity Style Book. Annual.
Philadelphia: Ayer Press.

Bibliography of Fund Raising and Philanthropy. George T.
Holloway, editor. New York: National Catholic Development Conference, 1975. 84p.

Borst, Diane, and Montana, Patrick J. , editors. Managing

17

Nonprofit Organizations. New York: Amacom, 1977. 328p.

Butners, Astrida, and Norman Buntaine. Motivations for Charitable Giving: A Reference Guide. Washington, D. C.: The 501 (c) (3) Group, 1973. 69p.

Carr, Elliot G. Better Management of Business Giving. Foreword by John H. Watson III. New York: Hobbs, Dorman, 1966. 114p.

Carter, Paul C. Handbook of Successful Fund-Raising. New York: Hawthorn, 1970. Various pagings.

Cary, William Lucius, and Craig B. Bright. The Developing Law of Endowment Funds: "The Law and the Lore" Revisited; Report to the Ford Foundation. New York: Ford Foundation, 1974. 56p.

Cary, William Lucius, and Craig B. Bright. The Law and the Lore of Endowment Funds; Report to the Ford Foundation. New York: Ford Foundation, 1969. 82p.

Chauncey, Charles F. "County Funding of the Arts in New York State; A Report of Money and Services Provided to Arts Organizations by the County Governments of New York State Outside New York City During 1975." New York: Office of Funding Assistance, New York State Council on the Arts, 1977. 24p.

Cleveland Area Arts Council. "'How-To' Guides for Publicity Chairpersons." Cleveland, 1973. 25p.

Cohen, Lily, and Oppendisano-Reich, Marie, editors. A National Guide to Government and Foundation Funding Sources in the Field of Aging. Garden City, N. Y.: Adelphi University Press, 1977. 174p.

Commerce Clearing House. The Private Foundation and the Tax Reform Act. Chicago, 1970. 157p.

Commission on Foundations and Private Philanthropy. Foundations, Public Giving, and Public Policy; Report and Recommendations. Chicago: University of Chicago Press, 1970. 287p.

The Commission on Private Philanthropy and Public Needs.

Giving in America; Toward a Stronger Voluntary Sector.
Washington, D. C. : 1975. 240p.

Conrad, Daniel Lynn. Techniques of Fund-Raising. Secaucus, N. J. : L. Stuart, 1974. 185p.

The Corporation and the Campus. Edited by Robert H. Con-
nery. New York: Praeger, 1970. 187p.

Council for Financial Aid to Education. "How to Develop and
Administer a Corporate Gift-Matching Program. " New
York: Council for Financial Aid to Education, n. d.
23p.

Cultural Directory: Guide to Federal Funds and Services for
Cultural Activities. Research conducted by Linda Coe.
New York: Associated Councils of the Arts, 1975.
356p. Originally published in 1971 under title, Washington and the Arts.

Cuninggim, Merrimon. Private Money and Public Service;
The Role of Foundations in American Society. New
York: McGraw-Hill, 1972. 267p.

Cutlip, Scott M. , and Allen H. Center. Effective Public Relations. 4th ed. Englewood Cliffs, N. J. : Prentice-
Hall, 1971. 701p.

Dermer, Joseph. The New How to Raise Funds from Foundations. 3d rev. ed. New York: Public Service Materials Center, 1975. 95p.

Dermer, Joseph, editor. Where America's Large Foundations
Make Their Grants. 2d ed. New York: Public Service
Materials Center, 1974. 256p.

Des Marais, Philip. How to Get Government Grants. New
York: Public Service Materials Center, 1975. 160p.

Dickinson, Frank G. The Changing Position of Philanthropy
in the American Economy. New York: National Bureau
of Economic Research, Columbia University Press,
1970. 222p.

Fisch, Edith L. ; Doris Jonas Freed, and Esther R. Schacter.
Charities and Charitable Foundations. Pomona, N. Y. :
Lond Publications, 1974. 869p.

Fondazione Giovanni Agnelli. Guide to European Foundations. Milan: Franco Angeli Editore, 1973; distributed by Columbia University Press. 401p.

Ford Foundation. Report. Annual. New York.

Foundation Center. The Foundation Center National Data Book, 1974-76. New York, 1977. 2 volumes.

Foundation Center. Foundation Grants to Individuals. New York, 1977. 227p.

Foundation Center. List of Organizations Filing as Private Foundations. New York, 1973; distributed by Columbia University Press. 167p.

Foundation Center Information Quarterly. The Foundation Center, New York. ceased publication. October 1972-July 1974; thereafter

Foundation Center Source Book Profiles. New York, 1977- ; distributed by Columbia University Press. Looseleaf.

Foundation Directory. 6th ed. Marianna O. Lewis, editor. New York: Foundation Center, 1977; distributed by Columbia University Press. 661p.

Foundation Grants Index: A Cumulative Listing of Foundation Grants. Annual. Lee Noe, grants editor. New York: Foundation Center. Updated in Foundation News.

Foundation News. Bi-monthly. Patrick W. Kennedy, editor. Council on Foundations, 888 Seventh Ave., New York, N. Y. 10019. Index. Circulation: 9000.

Fremont-Smith, Marion R. Philanthropy and the Business Corporation. New York: Russell Sage Foundation, 1972. 110p.

Fund Raising Management. Bi-monthly. John McIlquham, editor; Henry R. Hoke, Jr., publisher. Garden City, N. Y.: Advertising, book reviews, illustrations. Circulation: 10,000.

The Future of Foundations. Fritz F. Heimann, editor. Englewood Cliffs, N. J.: Prentice-Hall, 1973. 278p.

Georgi, Charlotte. Foundations, Grants & Fund-Raising; A Selected Bibliography. Los Angeles: Graduate School of Management, University of California, 1976. 67p.

Giving USA. Annual. New York: American Association of Fund Raising Counsel.

Goulden, Joseph C. The Money Givers. New York: Random House, 1971. 341p.

The Grants Register. Bienniel. New York: St. Martin's Press.

Grantsmanship Center News. 8 issues per year. Thomas T. Whitney, editor. Grantsmanship Center, Los Angeles, Calif. 90015. Book reviews, index. Circulation: 10, 500.

"Grantsmanship: Money and How to Get It." Orange, N. J. : Academic Media, 1973. 27p.

Hall, Mary. Developing Skills in Proposal Writing. Corvallis, Ore. : Continuing Education Publications, 1971. 194p.

Hardy, James M. Corporate Planning for Nonprofit Organizations. New York: Association Press, 1973. 119p.

Harris, James F. , and Anne Klepper. Corporate Philanthropic Public Service Activities. New York: Conference Board, 1976. 61p.

Hillman, Howard, and Karin Abarbanel. The Art of Winning Foundation Grants. New York: Vanguard Press, 1975. 188p.

Holder, Jack J. Corporate Support Programs to Institutions of Higher Learning. Danville, Ill. : Interstate Printers and Publishers, 1967. 161p.

Humphries, H. R. Fund Raising for Small Charities and Organizations. Newton Abbot, England: David and Charles, 1972. 124p.

Hunter, Thomas Willard. The Tax Climate for Philanthropy. Washington, D. C. : American College Public Relations Association, 1968. 207p.

Institute of International Education. International Awards in the Arts; For Graduate and Professional Study. New York: Institute of International Education, 1969. 105p.

The International Foundation Directory. H. V. Hodson, consultant editor. Detroit: Gale Research Company, 1974. 396p.

Katz, Harvey. Give! Who Gets Your Charity Dollar? Garden City, N. Y.: Doubleday, 1974. 252p.

LaHoud, John. Theater Reawakening: A Report on Ford Foundation Assistance to American Drama. New York: Ford Foundation, 1977. 44p.

Liebert, Edwin R. and Bernice E. Sheldon. Handbook of Special Events for Nonprofit Organizations; Tested Ideas for Fund Raising and Public Relations. With a foreword by David M. Church. New York: Association Press, 1972. 224p.

Martinson, Jean Ann, comp. International Philanthropy: A Compilation of Grants by United States Foundations. New York: The Foundation Center, 1977. 213p.

Metropolitan Cultural Alliance. Getting in Ink and on the Air: A Publicity Handbook. Boston, 1973. 48p.

Miller, Thomas F., and Orser, G. R. "You Don't Know What You Got Until You Lose It: An Introduction to Accounting, Budgeting and Tax Planning for Small, Nonprofit Organizations and Community Groups." Washington, D. C.: The Support Center/The Community Management Center, 1975. 31p.

Nason, John W. Trustees and the Future of Foundations. New York: Council on Foundations, 1977. 112p.

National Council on the Arts. National Endowment for the Arts. The First Five Years: Fiscal 1966 Through Fiscal 1970. Washington, D. C.: National Council on the Arts. Various pagings.

National Directory of Grants and Aid to Individuals in the Arts, International. 3d ed. By Daniel Millsaps and the editors of the Washington International Arts Letter. Washington, D. C.: Washington International Arts Letter, 1976. 221p.

National Endowment for the Arts. Annual Report. Washington, D. C. : U. S. Government Printing Office.

National Endowment for the Arts. Guide to Programs. Annual. Washington, D. C.

National Endowment for the Arts. "Research Division Program Solicitation--Study of the Condition and Needs of the American Theatre. " Washington, D. C. , 1977. 35p.

National Endowment for the Humanities. Program Announcement. Annual. Washington, D. C.

Nelson, Ralph L. Economic Factors in the Growth of Corporation Giving. New York: National Bureau of Economic Research and Russell Sage Foundation, 1970. 116p. (National Bureau of Economic Research Occasional Paper 111.)

Nelson, Ralph L. The Investment Policies of Foundations. New York: Russell Sage Foundation, 1967. 203p.

New York (State). State University. Washington Office. Support for the Arts; A Survey of Possible Sources for State University of New York. Susan G. Sorrels, editor. Washington, D. C. , 1973. 164p.

Newton, Michael, and Scott Hatley. Persuade and Provide; The Story of the Arts and Education Council in St. Louis. New York: Associated Councils of the Arts, 1970. 249p.

Nielsen, Waldemar A. The Big Foundations. New York: Columbia University Press, 1972. 475p.

Patrick, Kenneth Gilbert, and Richard Eells. Education and the Business Dollar; A Study of Corporate Contributions Policy and American Education. New York: Macmillan, 1969. 313p.

Peterson, Eric. Nonprofit Arts Organizations: Formation and Maintenance. Berkeley, Calif. : Bay Area Lawyers for the Arts, 1977. 175p.

Petroff, John. The Charitable Remainder Trust--Is There a Better Way to Make a Large Donation? New York: New York University, Graduate School of Business Ad-

ministration, Institute of Finance, 1974. (Special issue
of The Bulletin, Numbers 96-97, April 1974.) 72p.

Philanthropy in the 70's: An Anglo-American Discussion. A
Report on the Anglo-American Conference on the Role
of Philanthropy in the 1970's, Ditchley Park, England,
April 28 to May 1, 1972. Edited by John J. Corson and
Harry V. Hodson. New York: Council on Foundations,
1973. 116p.

Pressment, Stanley. What You Must Know to Manage a Charitable Foundation Under the Tax Reform Act. Greenvale,
N.Y., n.d. Looseleaf.

Private Foundations and Business Corporations Active in
Arts/Humanities/Education. By Daniel Millsaps and editors of the Washington International Arts Letter. Washington, D.C.: Washington International Arts Letter, v.
1 1970, 138p.; v. 2 1974, 264p.

Reeves, Thomas C., compiler. Foundations Under Fire.
Ithaca, N.Y.: Cornell University Press, 1970. 235p.

Richman, Saul. Public Information Handbook for Foundations.
Foreword by Robert F. Goheen. New York: Council
on Foundations, 1973. 95p.

Robinson, Susan Clark; Patricia Tobey, and Mary Anna Col-
well. A Guide to California Foundations. Burlingame,
Calif.: San Mateo Foundation, 1976.

Rudy, William H. The Foundations, Their Use and Abuse.
Washington, D.C.: Public Affairs Press, 1970. 75p.

Shapiro, Benson P. Marketing in Nonprofit Organizations.
Cambridge, Mass.: Marketing Science Institute, 1972.
47p.

Taft Products. The Proposal Writer's Swipe File: Twelve
Professionally Written Grant Proposals--Prototypes of
Approaches, Styles and Structures. Jean Brodsky, edi-
tor. Washington, D.C., 1973. 135p.

Tax Impacts on Philanthropy. By Douglas Dillon and others.
Symposium conducted by the Tax Institute of America,
Dec. 2-3, 1971, Washington, D.C. Princeton, N.J.:
Tax Institute of America, 1972. 234p.

Tax Problems of Non-Profit Organizations. 14 papers pre-
        sented at the Fourth Annual American University Confer-
        ence on Federal Tax Problems of Non-Profit Organiza-
        tions, held in Washington, D.C., February, 1968. Edi-
        ted by George D. Webster. New York: Journal of Tax-
        ation, 1968. 265p.

Traub, Jack. Accounting and Reporting Practices of Private
        Foundations: A Critical Evaluation. New York: Prae-
        ger, 1977. 240p.

U.S. Library of Congress. Education and Public Welfare
        Division. Millions for the Arts: Federal and State Cul-
        tural Programs; An Exhaustive Senate Report. Washing-
        ton, D.C.: Washington International Arts Letter, 1972.
        58p.

U.S. Social and Rehabilitation Service. Grants Administra-
        tion Policies. Washington, D.C.: U.S. Government
        Printing Office, 1972. 53p.

The Volunteer Urban Consulting Group. Recruiting Business
        Executives for the Boards of Directors on Nonprofit Or-
        ganizations. New York: Volunteer Urban Consulting
        Group, 1977. 52p.

Warner, Irving R. The Art of Fund Raising. New York:
        Harper & Row, 1975. 176p.

Wayne, June. "Foundation Gamesmanship." A symposium
        sponsored by the California Arts Commission in coopera-
        tion with Continuing Education in Health Sciences, Uni-
        versity of California San Francisco Medical Center, St.
        Francis Hotel, San Francisco, May 21 and 22, 1966.
        Los Angeles: Tamarind Lithography Workshop, 1966.
        13p.

"While You're Up, Get Me a Grant: A Basic Bibliography on
        Grants." San Francisco: Bay Area Social Responsibili-
        ties Round Table, 1976. 10p.

Whitaker, Benjamin Charles George. The Philanthropoids:
        Foundations and Society; Unsubsidized Anatomy of the
        Burden of Benevolence. New York: Morrow, 1974.
        256p.

White, Stephen. "Evaluation of Foundation Activities." New
        York: Alfred P. Sloan Foundation, 1970. 15p.

White, Virginia P. Grants: How to Find Out about Them and What to Do Next. New York: Plenum Press, 1975. 354p.

Young, Donald R., and Wilbert E. Moore. Trusteeship and the Management of Foundations. New York: Russell Sage Foundation, 1969. 158p.

Zurcher, Arnold J., and Jane Dustan. The Foundation Administrator; A Study of Those Who Manage America's Foundations. New York: Russell Sage Foundation, 1972. 171p.

Zurcher, Arnold J., and Jane Dustan. Management of American Foundations: Administration, Policies and Social Role. New York: New York University Press, 1972. 184p.

IV

GOVERNMENT AND THE ARTS

Ad Hoc Coalition of States for the Arts in Education. Comprehensive Arts Planning. New York: coordinated by the JDR 3d Fund, 1975. 111p.

Adams, William H. The Politics of Art; Forming a State Arts Council. New York: Arts Councils of America, 1966. 49p.

Arey, June Batten. State Arts Agencies in Transition: Purpose, Program, and Personnel. Wayzata, Minn.: Spring Hill Conference Center, 1975. 267p.

Arts Council of Great Britain. Annual Report. London.

Arts in Society. Entire issue: Government and the Arts, v. 2, no. 4, Fall-Winter 1963-64.

Arts in Society. Entire issue: The Politics of Art, v. 10, no. 3, Fall-Winter 1973.

Associated Councils of the Arts. Cities, Counties and the Arts. New York, 1976. 44p.

Associated Councils of the Arts. A Guide to Community Arts Agencies. Edited by Michael K. Newton and Barbara B. Israel. New York, 1974. 373p.

Associated Councils of the Arts. State Arts Councils. New York, 1972. 80p.

Burgard, Ralph. Arts in the City; Organizing and Programming Community Arts Councils. New York: Associated Councils of the Arts, 1968. 150p.

California. Arts Commission. The Arts in California; A

Report to the Governor and the Legislature on the Cultural and Artistic Resources of the State of California. Sacramento, 1966. 86p.

Canadian Conference of the Arts. Direction Canada; A Declaration of Canadian Cultural Concern. Toronto, 1973. 78p.

Chauncey, Charles F. "County Funding of the Arts in New York State; A Report of Money and Services Provided to Arts Organizations by the County Governments of New York State Outside New York City During 1975. " New York: Office of Funding Assistance, New York State Council on the Arts, 1977. 24p.

Cultural Directory: Guide to Federal Funds and Services for Cultural Activities. Research conducted by Linda Coe. New York: Associated Councils of the Arts, 1975. 356p. (Originally published in 1971 under title, Washington and the Arts.)

Cwi, David, and Albert Diehl. In Search of a Regional Policy for the Arts. Baltimore: Joint Committee on Cultural Resources, 1975. 186p.

Emery, Walter Byron. Broadcasting and Government; Responsibilities and Regulations. Rev. ed. East Lansing: Michigan State University, 1971. 569p.

Fort Wayne Fine Arts Foundation. "A Proposal to Establish a Community Arts School. " Prepared by Concerned Citizens of Fort Wayne, Indiana. Fort Wayne, 1972. 32p.

Green, Dennis. % For Art: New Legislation Can Integrate Art and Architecture. Edited by Brennan Rash. Denver: Western States Arts Foundation, 1976. 72p.

Harris, John S. Government Patronage of the Arts in Great Britain. Chicago: University of Chicago Press, 1970. 341p.

Housing for Artists: The New York Experience. Prepared by Willkie Farr & Gallagher. New York: Volunteer Lawyers for the Arts, 1976. Various pagings.

Illinois. Advisory Commission on Financing the Arts in Illinois. Report. Chicago, 1971. 129p.

Johnson, Priscilla. Khrushchev and the Arts: The Politics of Soviet Culture, 1962-1964. Cambridge, Mass.: MIT Press, 1965. 300p.

Krawitz, Herman E., with Howard K. Klein. Royal American Symphonic Theater: A Radical Proposal for a Subsidized Professional Theater. New York: Macmillan, 1975. 211p.

McDonald, William Francis. Federal Relief Administration and the Arts; The Origins and Administrative History of the Works Project Administration. Columbus: Ohio University Press, 1969. 869p.

Minihan, Janet. The Nationalization of Culture: The Development of State Subsidies to the Arts in Great Britain. New York: New York University Press, 1976. 276p.

National Council on the Arts. National Endowment for the Arts. The First Five Years: Fiscal 1966 Through Fiscal 1970. Washington, D.C.: National Council on the Arts. Various pagings.

National Directory for the Performing Arts and Civic Centers. Edited by Beatrice Handel, Janet Spencer and Nolanda Turner. Dallas: Handel, 1975. 972p.

National Endowment for the Arts. Annual Report. Washington, D.C.: U.S. Government Printing Office.

National Endowment for the Arts. Guide to Programs. Annual. Washington, D.C.: U.S. Government Printing Office.

National Endowment for the Arts. Office of Research. Federal Funds and Services for the Arts. Compiled by Judith G. Gault for the Office of Education, U.S. Department of Health, Education and Welfare. Washington, D.C.: U.S. Government Printing Office, 1967.

National Endowment for the Humanities. Annual Report. Washington, D.C.: U.S. Government Printing Office.

National Endowment for the Humanities. Program Announcement. Annual. Washington, D.C.: U.S. Government Printing Office.

National Research Center of the Arts. A Study of the Nonprofit Arts and Cultural Industry of New York State. New York, 1972. 194p.

New York (City). Mayor's Committee on Cultural Policy. Report of the Mayor's Committee on Cultural Policy, October 15, 1974. New York, 1974. 87p.

New York (State). Commission on Cultural Resources. Cultural Resource Development. New York: Praeger, 1976. 219p.

New York (State). State Council on the Arts. New York State Council on the Arts: Report. Annual. New York.

New York. State University. Washington Office. Support for the Arts; A Survey of Possible Sources for State University of New York. Susan G. Sorrels, editor. Washington, D.C., 1973. 164p.

O'Connor, Francis V. Federal Support for the Visual Arts: The New Deal and Now; A Report on the New Deal Art Projects in New York City and State with Recommendations for Present-day Federal Support for the Visual Arts to the National Endowment for the Arts. Greenwich, Conn.: New York Graphic Society, 1969. 226p.

O'Connor, Francis V., editor. The New Deal Art Projects: An Anthology of Memoirs. Washington, D.C.: Smithsonian Institution Press, 1972.

Pasquill, Frank T., and Joan Horsman. Wooden Pennies: A Report on Cultural Funding Patterns in Canada. Toronto: York University, Programme in Arts Administration, 1973. 75p.

Popenoe, David, compiler. The Urban-Industrial Frontier; Essays on Social Trends and Industrial Goals in Modern Communities. New Brunswick, N.J.: Rutgers University, 1969. 176p. (See chapter, "Government, the Arts, and the City," by August Heckscher.)

Rivkin, Steven R. Cable Television: A Guide to Federal Regulations. New York: Crane, Russak, 1974. 370p.

Scott, Mellier Goodin. The States and the Arts; The California Arts Commission and the Emerging Federal-State Partnership. Berkeley: Institute of Governmental Studies, University of California, 1971. 129p.

State Financial Assistance to Cultural Resources; Report of the New York State Commission on Cultural Resources. New York: State Commission on Cultural Resources, 1971. 163p.

U. S. Library of Congress. Congressional Research Service. Survey of United States and Foreign Government Support for Cultural Activities. By Lilla M. Pearce. Prepared for the Special Subcommittee on Arts and Humanities of the Committee on Labor and Public Welfare, United States Senate. Washington, D. C. : U. S. Government Printing Office, 1971. 245p.

U. S. Library of Congress. Educational and Public Welfare Division. Millions for the Arts: Federal and State Cultural Programs. Washington, D. C. : Washington International Arts Letter, 1972. 58p.

U. S. Office of Education. "Support for the Arts and Humanities. " Washington, D. C. : U. S. Government Printing Office, 1972. 22p.

Video Resources in New York State. Prepared by the Film and Video Bureau with support from the New York State Council on the Arts. New York: Publishing Center for Cultural Resources, 1975. 64p.

V

LABOR UNIONS AND THE ARTS

Art Workers News. Monthly, 10 issues per year. Foundation for the Community of Artists, 32 Union Square
East, New York, N. Y. 10003. Advertising, book reviews, bibliographies, illustrations. Circulation:
10, 000. Tabloid format. Formerly Art Workers Newsletter.

Bernstein, Irving. The Economics of Television Film Production and Distribution; A Report to Screen Actors
Guild, February 8, 1960. Sherman Oaks, Calif. , 1960.
132p.

Bernstein, Irving. Hollywood at the Crossroads; An Economic
Study of the Motion Picture Industry, Especially Prepared for the Hollywood A F of L Film Council. Hollywood, Calif. , 1957. 78p.

Broadcasting and Bargaining; Labor Relations in Radio and
Television. Edited by Allen E. Koenig. Madison: University of Wisconsin Press, 1970. 334p.

Cauble, John R. "A Study of the International Alliance of
Theatrical Stage Employees and Moving Picture Machine
Operators of the United States and Canada. " Master's
thesis, University of California Los Angeles, 1964.
153p.

Directory of National Unions and Employee Associations.
Biennial. Washington, D. C. : U. S. Bureau of Labor
Statistics.

Faine, Hyman R. "Unions and the Arts. " Los Angeles:
Graduate School of Management, University of California,
1972. 17p. (Management in the Arts Research Paper
no. 11.)

Kleingartner, Archie, and Kenneth Lloyd. "A Note on Labor-Management Relations in the Performing Arts: The Case of Los Angeles." Los Angeles: Graduate School of Management, University of California, 1971. 12p. (Management in the Arts Research Paper no. 16.)

Kort, Michele F. "White Collar Unions in Art Museums: The Collective Response." Comprehensive research paper for UCLA Management in the Arts Program, Graduate School of Management, University of California, Los Angeles, 1974. 85p.

Lloyd, Kenneth. "Adherence to Work Rules: A Case Study of the Professional Theatrical Actor in the Los Angeles Area." Ph. D. dissertation, University of California, Los Angeles, 1972. 246p.

Moskow, Michael H. Labor Relations in the Performing Arts; An Introductory Survey. Foreword by John T. Dunlop. New York: Associated Councils of the Arts, 1969. 218p.

Screen Actors Guild. "The Story of the Screen Actors Guild." Hollywood, Calif.: Public Relations Department, Screen Actors Guild, 1966. 23p.

Stoyle, Judith. Economic and Demographic Characteristics of Actors' Equity Association Membership. Philadelphia: Actors' Equity Association in cooperation with Bureau of Economic and Business Research, School of Business Administration, Temple University of the Commonwealth System of Higher Education, 1970.

Wertheimer, Barbara M. Exploring the Arts; A Handbook for Trade Union Program Planners. New York: New York State School of Industrial and Labor Relations, Cornell University, Division of Extension and Public Service, 1968. 61p.

VI

LEGAL ASPECTS OF THE ARTS

Adams, Laurie. Art Cop, Robert Volpe: Art Crime Detective. New York: Dodd, Mead, 1974. 240p.

American Institute of Certified Public Accountants. Accounting Standards Subcommittee on Nonprofit Organizations. "Discussion Draft: Tentative Set of Accounting Principles and Reporting Practices for Nonprofit Organizations Not Covered by Existing AICPA Industry Audit Guides. " New York, 1977. 28p.

Art Works: Law, Policy, Practice. Edited by Franklin Feldman and Stephen E. Weil. New York: Practising Law Institute, 1974. 1241p.

Arts Advocate. Quarterly, membership. Advocates for the Arts, c/o John Hightower, chairman, Room 820, 1564 Broadway, New York, N.Y. 10036

Berk, Lee Eliot. Legal Protection for the Creative Musician. Boston: Berklee Press, 1970. 371p.

Beverly Hills Bar Association. Program on Legal Aspects of the Entertainment Industry. Annual. Cosponsored with the University of Southern California Law Center, Los Angeles, 1958- . The following volumes are recommended especially:

11. Television film production and distribution; 1 vol. , 1965; various pagings.
13. Current industry developments. Topic: Artists' managers, personal managers, and business managers: their functions in the entertainment field. 1 vol. , 1967; various pagings.
14. Production money (where the money is and what

the money gets). Topics: Financing independent motion picture and television projects, financing independent phonograph record production, foreign film subsidies and other state aids as an aspect of financing, financing entertainment vehicles under the Uniform Commercial Code; 1 vol. , 1968; various pagings.

15. Current industry developments. Topic 1--Cable television: technology and the law; 2--First amendment developments in the law of privacy; 3--Disney's integrated marketing and licensing approach; 1 vol. , 1969; various pagings.

17. Syllabus and forms on percentage deals in the motion picture, television, music and recording industries; edited by Michael Harris, 1971; various pagings.

18. Forms of agreement for purchase and sale transactions in the motion picture, television, phonograph recording and music publishing industries; edited by Michael Harris, 1 vol. , 1972; various pagings.

19. Syllabus and forms on personal service agreements revisited: motion pictures and television; edited by Owen J. Sloane and Richard A. Rosenberg, 1973; 288p.

20. Syllabus and forms on non-studio and other novel sources and methods of financing motion pictures; edited by Richard A. Rosenberg and Owen J. Sloane, 1974; 291p.

Carmen, Ira R. Movies, Censorship, and the Law. Ann Arbor: University of Michigan Press, 1966. 399p.

Connaughton, Howard W. Craftsmen in Business: A Guide to Financial Management and Taxes. New York: American Crafts Council, 1975. 73p.

Counseling Clients in the Performing Arts, 1976. Gerald A. Margolis and Martin E. Silfen, cochairmen. New York: Practising Law Institute, 1976. 384p.

Crawford, Tad. Legal Guide for the Visual Artist. New York: Hawthorn Books, 1977. 257p.

DeGrazia, Edward. Censorship Landmarks. New York: Bowker, 1969. 657p.

DuBoff, Leonard David. Art Law, Domestic and International. South Hackensack, N. J. : F. B. Rothman, 1975. 627p.

Federal Bar Association of New York, New Jersey and Connecticut. Committee on the Law of the Theatre. The Business and Law of Music; A Symposium. Edited by Joseph Taubman. New York: Federal Legal Publications, 1965. 111p.

Federal Bar Association of New York, New Jersey and Connecticut. Financing a Theatrical Production; A Symposium. Edited by Joseph Taubman. New York: Federal Legal Publications, 1964. 499p.

Hodes, Scott. What Every Artist and Collector Should Know About the Law. New York: Dutton, 1974. 268p.

Holcomb, Bill. Fear of Filing: A Beginner's Handbook for Dancers and Other Artists on Record Keeping and Federal Taxes. New York: Volunteer Lawyers for the Arts, 1975. Various pagings.

Index to Legal Periodicals. Monthly, October-August; annual and three-year cumulations. H. W. Wilson Co. , 950 University Ave. , The Bronx, N. Y. 10452. (An author and subject index to legal periodicals and journals.)

Kaplan, Benjamin, and Ralph S. Brown, Jr. Cases on Copyright, Unfair Competition, and Other Topics Bearing on the Protection of Literary, Musical, and Artistic Works. 2d ed. Mineola, N. Y. : The Foundation Press, 1974. 997p.

Kintner, Earl Wilson, and Jack L. Lahr. An Intellectual Property Law Primer: A Survey of the Law of Patents, Trade Secrets, Trademarks, Franchises, Copyrights, and Personality and Entertainment Rights. New York: Macmillan, 1975. 539p.

Law and the Visual Arts Conference, Portland, Oregon, 1974. Law and the Visual Arts. Edited by Leonard D. DuBoff and Mary Ann Crawford DuBoff. Portland, Ore. : DuBoff, 1974. 359p. (Sponsored by the Northwestern School of Law of Lewis and Clark College.)

Legal and Business Problems of Artists, Art Galleries and Museums; Sources and Materials. Franklin Feldman,

Stephen E. Weil, cochairmen. New York: Practising
Law Institute, 1973. 712p.

Legal and Business Problems of Television and Radio, 1973.
Harry R. Olsson, chairman. New York: Practising
Law Institute, 1973. 608p.

Legal and Business Problems of the Motion Picture Industry.
Paul A. Baumgarten, chairman. New York: Practising
Law Institute, 1973. 616p.

Legal and Business Problems of the Record Industry. Donald
E. Biederman, chairman. New York: Practising Law
Institute, 1974. 536p.

Lidstone, Herrick K. Exempt Organizations and the Arts.
New York: Volunteer Lawyers for the Arts, 1975.
38p.

Lidstone, Herrick K. The Individual Artist: Record Keeping,
Methods of Accounting, Income and Itemized Deductions
for Federal Income Tax Purposes. New York: Volunteer Lawyers for the Arts, 1976. 52p.

Lindey, Alexander. Entertainment, Publishing and the Arts--
Agreements and the Law. New York: Clark Boardman,
1963- . 2 volumes, looseleaf.

McClellan, Grant S. , compiler. Censorship in the United
States. New York: H. W. Wilson Co. , 1967. 222p.
(The Reference Shelf, v. 39, no. 3.)

Mayer, Michael F. The Film Industries; Practical Business/
Legal Problems in Production, Distribution, and Exhibition. New York: Hastings House, 1973. 212p.

Middlemas, Robert Keith. The Double Market: Art Theft and
Art Thieves. Farnborough, England: Saxon House,
1975. 237p.

Miller, Thomas F. and Orser, G. R. "You Don't Know What
You Got Until You Lose It: An Introduction to Account-
ing, Budgeting and Tax Planning for Small, Nonprofit
Organizations and Community Groups. " Washington, D. C. :
The Support Center/The Community Management Center,
1975. 31p.

Moon, Eric, editor. Book Selection and Censorship in the Sixties. New York: R. R. Bowker, 1969. 421p.

Nimmer, Melville B. Nimmer on Copyright; A Treatise on the Law of Literary, Musical and Artistic Property, and the Protection of Ideas. Albany, N. Y. : Mathew Bender, 1963- . Looseleaf.

Noll, Roger G.; Merton J. Peck, and John J. McGowan. Economic Aspects of Television Regulation. Washington, D. C. : Brookings Institution, 1973. 342p.

Parker, Ben R. , and Pat J. Drabik. Creative Intention. New York: Law-Arts Publishers, 1972. 292p.

Price, Monroe E. Government Policy and Economic Security for Artists: The Case of the "Droit de Suite. " Los Angeles, 1970. 70p.

Randall, Richard S. Censorship of the Movies; The Social and Political Control of a Mass Medium. Madison: University of Wisconsin Press, 1968. 280p.

Rivkin, Steven R. Cable Television: A Guide to Federal Regulations. New York: Crane, Russak, 1974. 390p.

Scott, Michael. The Crafts Business Encyclopedia: Marketing, Management, and Money. New York: Harcourt Brace Jovanovich, 1977. 286p.

Spiegel, Irwin O. , and Jay L. Cooper, compilers and editors. Record and Music Publishing Forms of Agreement in Current Use. New York: Law-Arts, 1971. Looseleaf.

Taubman, Joseph. Performing Arts: Management and Law. New York: Law-Arts Publishers, 1973. 4 volumes with supplements.

Traub, Jack. Accounting and Reporting Practices of Private Foundations: A Critical Evaluation. New York: Praeger, 1977. 240p.

The Visual Artist and the Law. Rev. ed. by Associated Councils of the Arts, the Association of the Bar of the City of New York, Volunteer Lawyers for the Arts. New York: Praeger, 1974. 87p.

Whicher, John F. The Creative Arts and the Judicial Process; Four Variations on a Legal Theme. New York: Federal Legal Publications, 1965. 252p.

VII

MANAGEMENT IN THE ARTS
PUBLICATIONS AND WORKING PAPERS*

1. Adizes, Ichak. "UCLA Conferences on Arts Administration: Summary of the Meetings and a Report on Implementation. " Los Angeles, 1969. 34p.

†2. Georgi, Charlotte. "The Arts and the Art of Administration; A Selected Bibliography. " Los Angeles, 1970. 51p.

3. "California Theater Index, 1971: College, University Facilities. " Los Angeles, 1971. 46p.

4. Adizes, Ichak. "The Unique Character of Performing Arts Organizations and the Functioning of Their Boards of Directors (a Managerial Analysis). " Los Angeles, 1971. 14p.

5. Adizes, Ichak. "Seattle Opera Association; A Policy Making Case for Management in the Arts. " Los Angeles, 1971. 53p.

6. Goodman, Richard Alan, and Mirta Samuelson. "An Exploration Into the Administrative Support of the Creative Process: The Theater Case. " Los Angeles, 1970. 13p.

7. Pfeffer, Irving. "Fine Arts: A Program in Risk Management. " Los Angeles, 1971. 34p.

---

*This is the name of a series published by the Management in the Arts Program, Graduate School of Management/Division of Research, University of California Los Angeles.
†Papers 2, 17, 23 and 33 are incorporated in the present bibliography.

8. Granfield, Michael. "The Live Performing Arts: Financial Catastrophe or Economic Catharsis." Los Angeles, 1971. 23p.

9. Adizes, Ichak, and William McWhinney. "Arts, Society and Administration: The Role and Training of Arts Administrators." Los Angeles, 1971. 16p.

10. Blaine, Martha. "The Parkview Symphony: Cases A and B." Los Angeles, 1971. 20p.

11. Faine, Hyman R. "Unions and the Arts." Los Angeles, 1972. 17p.

12. Garrison, Lee C. "The Composition, Attendance Behavior and Needs of Motion Picture Audiences: A Review of the Literature." Los Angeles, 1971. 36p.

13. Garrison, Lee C., and Christina Vogl Kaali-Nagy. "Comparative Profiles of Users and Nonusers of the Los Angeles Music Center." Los Angeles, 1971. 38p.

14. Goodman, Richard Alan, and Lawrence Peter Goodman. "Theatre as a Temporary System." Los Angeles, 1971. 15p.

15. Adizes, Ichak. "Administering for the Arts--Problems in Practice." Los Angeles, 1971.

16. Kleingartner, Archie, and Kenneth Lloyd. "A Note on Labor-Management Relations in the Performing Arts: The Case of Los Angeles." Los Angeles, 1971. 12p.

†17. Georgi, Charlotte. "Management and the Arts: A Selected Bibliography." Los Angeles, 1972. 51p.

18. McWhinney, William H., and James M. Woods. "A Curator for the Future." Los Angeles, 1972. 11p.

19. McWhinney, William H., and James M. Woods. "Arts in the Neighborhood." Los Angeles, 1973. 22p.

20. McWhinney, William H., and James M. Woods. "Should I Have Given Them My Card? Comments on Art

Education for the Minorities. " Los Angeles, 1974.
13p.

21. Faine, Hy, and Sid L. Conrad. "Politics of the Arts:
Evolving Issues and Present Conflicts and Proceed-
ings of UCLA Colloquium on the Politics of the Arts:
The Public Sector; Minorities and the Arts; The
Private Sector. " In Arts in Society, v. 10, no. 3,
Fall-Winter, 1973.

22. Goodman, Richard A. , and Lawrence P. Goodman.
"Professional Development and Effective Manpower
Utilization in Temporary Systems: The Theatre
Case. " Los Angeles, 1974. Various pagings.

†23. Georgi, Charlotte. "The Arts and the World of Business:
A Selected Bibliography (Supplement I). " Los Angeles, 1974. 64p.

24. Hutchinson, William. "General Value Theory and Arts
Management. " Los Angeles, 1974. 20p.

25. Adizes, Ichak. "The Cost of Being An Artist, " in California Management Review, v. 17, no. 4, Summer
1975.

26. Hutchinson, William. "Arts Management and the Art
of Music, " in Arts in Society, v. 12, no. 1, Spring /
Summer 1975.

27. Bolan, Robert S. "The Impact of Foundation Support
on Creativity in the Performing Arts. " Los Angeles, 1975.

28. McEvoy, Annette, under the supervision of Thomas Copeland. "Financial Planning for Performing Arts Organizations. " Los Angeles, 1975.

29. Kort, Michele, and Jacquelyn Maguire. "Tenure in
Museums. " Los Angeles, 1974. 14p. (A shorter
version of this paper appears in Museum News,
v. 53, no. 4, December 1974.)

30. "Administering for the Arts, " in California Management
Review, v. 15, no. 2, Winter 1972. (Special section comprising research papers 4, 7, 13, 14, 15
[edited version], and 16.)

31. Osborne, Alfred E. "Economics of the Performing Arts: A Bibliography (Mainly Theater). " Los Angeles, 1976.

32. Denton, Mark; Ruth Goldstein, and Cheryl Yuen. "Funding for the Arts. " Los Angeles, 1976.

†33. Georgi, Charlotte. "The Arts and the World of Business: A Selected Bibliography (Supplement II). " Los Angeles, 1976, 67p.

[Unnumbered] Kort, Michele F. "White-Collar Unions in Art Museums: the Collective Response. " Los Angeles, 1974. 85p. (Comprehensive research paper for the UCLA Management in the Arts Program.)

VIII

THE MASS MEDIA:
RADIO, TELEVISION, AND FILMS

Arts in Society. Entire issue: Film: New Challenge and
New Possibility, v. 10, no. 2, Summer-Fall 1973.

Audiovisual Market Place: A Multimedia Guide. Annual.
New York: Bowker.

Baker, Fred, with Ross Firestone. Movie People; At Work
in the Business of Film. New York: Douglas Book
Corp. , 1972. 193p.

Balio, Tino. United Artists: The Company Built by the
Stars. Madison: University of Wisconsin Press, 1976.
323p.

Baumgarten, Paul A. , and Donald C. Farber. Producing,
Financing and Distributing Film. New York: Drama
Book Specialists, 1973. 198p.

Bernstein, Irving. The Economics of Television Film Production and Distribution; A Report to Screen Actors
Guild, February 8, 1960. Sherman Oaks, Calif. : 1960.
132p.

Bernstein, Irving. Hollywood at the Crossroads; An Econo-
mic Study of the Motion Picture Industry, Especially
Prepared for the Hollywood A F of L Film Council.
Hollywood, Calif. : 1957. 78p.

Beverly Hills Bar Association. Program on Legal Aspects
of the Entertainment Industry. (See entry under Part
VI, Legal Aspects of the Arts.)

Billboard. Weekly. Edited by Lee Zhito. Billboard Publi-

cations, Inc. , 9000 Sunset Blvd. , Los Angeles, Calif.
90069. Advertising; book, film, play, record, and television reviews; illustrations. Circulation: 35,339.

Bluem, A. William, and Jason E. Squire. The Movie Business; American Film Industry Practice. New York:
Hastings House, 1972. 368p. (Studies in Media Management.)

Blum, Eleanor. Basic Books in the Mass Media; An Annotated, Selected Booklist Covering General Communications,
Book Publishing, Broadcasting, Film, Magazines, Newspapers, Advertising, Indexes, and Scholarly and Professional Periodicals. Urbana: University of Illinois,
1972. 252p.

Bogart, Leo. The Age of Television; A Study of Viewing
Habits and the Impact of Television on American Life.
3d ed. New York: Frederick Ungar Pub. Co. , 1971.
515p.

Broadcasting and Bargaining; Labor Relations in Radio and
Television. Edited by Allen E. Koenig. Madison:
University of Wisconsin, 1970. 344p.

Broadcasting Cable Sourcebook. Annual. Washington, D. C. :
Broadcasting Publications.

Broadcasting Yearbook. Annual. Washington, D. C. : Broadcasting Publications.

Brown, Les. Television; The Business Behind the Box. New
York: Harcourt Brace Jovanovich, 1971. 374p.

Brown, William O. Low Budget Features. Hollywood, Calif. :
author, 1971. 231p. (Dealer: Larry Edmunds, 6658
Hollywood Blvd. , Los Angeles.)

Burder, John. The Work of the Industrial Film Maker. New
York: Hastings House, 1973. 255p.

Cantor, Muriel G. The Hollywood TV Producer; His Work
and His Audience. New York: Basic Books, 1971.
256p.

Carmen, Ira R. Movies, Censorship, and the Law. Ann
Arbor: University of Michigan Press, 1966. 399p.

Cauble, John R. "A Study of the International Alliance of Theatrical Stage Employees and Moving Picture Machine Operators of the United States and Canada." Master's thesis, University of California Los Angeles, 1964. 153p.

Center Theatre Group. Box Office Guidelines. New York: Foundation for the Extension and Development of the American Professional Theatre, 1974. 44p.

Cherington, Paul W.; Leo V. Hirsch, and Robert Brandwein. Television Station Ownership; A Case Study of Federal Agency Regulation. New York: Hastings House, 1971. 304p.

Cleveland Area Arts Council. "'How-To' Guides for Publicity Chairpersons." Cleveland, 1973. 25p.

Coddington, Robert H. Modern Radio Broadcasting: Management & Operation in Small-to-Medium Markets. Blue Ridge Summit, Pa.: G/L Tab Books, 1969. 256p.

Coleman, Howard W. Case Studies in Broadcast Management. New York: Hastings House, 1970. 95p.

Committee for Economic Development. Broadcasting and Cable Television: Policies for Diversity and Change. New York, 1975. 119p.

Costa, Sylvia Allen. How to Prepare a Production Budget for Film & Video Tape. 2d ed. Blue Ridge Summit, Pa.: Tab Books, 1975. 192p.

Costner, Tom. Motion Picture Market Place, 1976-1977. Boston: Little, Brown, 1976. 513p.

Davis, Clive, with James Willwerth. Clive: Inside the Record Business. New York: Morrow, 1974. 300p.

Degand, Claude. Le Cinéma ... Cette Industrie. Saint-Etienne: Editions Techniques et Economiques, 1972. 272p.

Diamant, Lincoln, editor. The Anatomy of a Television Commercial. New York: Hastings House, 1970. 191p.

Directors at Work; Interviews with American Film-Makers.

Interviews conducted and edited by Bernard R. Kantor, Irwin R. Blacker and Anne Kramer. New York: Funk and Wagnalls, 1970. 442p.

Eames, John Douglas. The MGM Story: The Complete History of Fifty Roaring Years. New York: Crown Publishers, 1975. 400p.

Easton, Carol. The Search for Sam Goldwyn. New York: Morrow, 1976. 304p.

Emery, Walter Byron. Broadcasting and Government: Responsibilities and Regulations. Rev. ed. East Lansing: Michigan State University, 1971. 569p.

Epstein, Edward Jay. News from Nowhere: Television and the News. New York: Random House, 1974. 321p.

Fadiman, William. Hollywood Now. New York: Liveright, 1972. 174p.

The Focal Encyclopedia of Film and Television Techniques. Edited by Raymonde Spottiswoode. New York: Hastings House, 1969. 1100p.

Garrison, Lee C. "The Composition, Attendance Behavior and Needs of Motion Picture Audiences: A Review of the Literature." Los Angeles: Graduate School of Management, University of California, 1971. 36p. (Management in the Arts Research Paper no. 12.)

Getting the Message Across: An Inquiry into Successes and Failures of Cross-Cultural Communication in the Contemporary World. New York: UNESCO Press, 1975. 214p.

Gordon, George N. The Communications Revolution: A History of Mass Media in the United States. New York: Hastings House, 1977.

Green, Timothy. The Universal Eye; The World of Television. New York: Stein & Day, 1972. 276p.

Greenfield, Jeff. Television: The First Fifty Years. New York: Abrams, 1977. 320p.

Guback, Thomas H. The International Film Industry; Western

Europe and America Since 1945. Bloomington: Indiana
University Press, 1969. 244p.

Head, Sydney W. Broadcasting in America. 2d ed. Boston:
Houghton Mifflin, 1972. 563p.

Higham, Charles. Warner Brothers. New York: Scribner's,
1975. 232p.

Hoffer, Jay. Managing Today's Radio Station. Blue Ridge
Summit, Pa.: G/L Tab Books, 1968. 288p.

Hoffer, Jay. Organization & Operation of Broadcast Stations.
Blue Ridge Summit, Pa.: G/L Tab Books, 1971.
251p.

Hoffer, Jay. Radio Production Techniques. Blue Ridge
Summit, Pa.: Tab Books, 1974. 192p.

International Index to Film Periodicals. Irregular. New
York: St. Martin's Press.

International Motion Picture Almanac. Annual. New York:
Quigley Publications.

International Television Almanac. Annual. New York: Quigley Publications.

Johnson, Joseph Steve, and Kenneth K. Jones. Modern Radio
Station Practices. Belmont, Calif.: Wadsworth Pub.
Co., 1972. 269p.

Jowett, Garth. Film: The Democratic Art. Boston: Little,
Brown, 1976. 518p.

Kaplan, Benjamin, and Ralph S. Brown, Jr. Cases on Copyright, Unfair Competition, and Other Topics Bearing on
the Protection of Literary, Musical, and Artistic Works.
2d ed. Mineola, N.Y.: Foundation Press, 1974.
997p.

Lahue, Kalton C. Motion Picture Pioneer: The Selig Poly-
scope Company. South Brunswick, N.J.: A. S. Barnes,
1973. 224p.

Lawton, Richard. A World of Movies: 70 Years of Film
History. London: Octopus Books, 1974. 383p.

Legal and Business Problems of Television and Radio, 1973.
 Harry R. Olsson, chairman. New York: Practising
 Law Institute, 1973. 608p.

Legal and Business Problems of the Motion Picture Industry.
 Paul A. Baumgarter, chairman. New York: Practising
 Law Institute, 1973. 616p.

Legal and Business Problems of the Record Industry. Donald
 E. Biederman, chairman. New York: Practising Law
 Institute, 1974. 536p.

Lindey, Alexander. Entertainment, Publishing and the Arts.
 New York: Clark Boardman, 1963- . 2 volumes, looseleaf.

Lyons, Timothy James. The Silent Partner: The History of
 the American Film Manufacturing Company, 1910-1921.
 New York: Arno Press, 1974. 256p.

Marx, Arthur. Goldwyn: A Biography of the Man Behind
 the Myth. New York: Norton, 1976. 376p.

Marx, Samuel. Mayer and Thalberg: The Make-Believe
 Saints. New York: Random House, 1975. 273p.

Mayer, Martin. About Television. New York: Harper and
 Row, 1972. 434p.

Mayer, Michael F. The Film Industries; Practical Business/
 Legal Problems in Production, Distribution, and Exhibition. New York: Hastings House, 1973. 212p.

Messick, Hank. The Beauties and the Beasts: The Mob in
 Show Business. New York: David McKay, 1973. 256p.

Method to the Madness (Hollywood Explained). Edited by
 Atkins and a cast of six. Livingston, N.J.: Prince
 Publishers, 1975. 207p.

Metropolitan Cultural Alliance. Getting in Ink and on the Air.
 Boston, 1973. 48p.

Metz, Robert. CBS: Reflections in a Bloodshot Eye. Chicago: Playboy Press, 1975. 428p.

Miller, D. Thomas. "Television: The Only Truly Mass

Medium Remaining Today: Its Role in Our Society. "
Ithaca, N. Y. : Department of Communication Arts, New
York State College of Agriculture and Life Sciences,
Cornell University, 1971. 11p.

Minus, Johnny, and William Storm Hale. The Movie Industry
Book; How Others Made and Lost Money in the Movie
Industry. Hollywood, Calif. : 7 Arts Press, 1970.
601p.

Mitchell, Curtis. Cavalcade of Broadcasting. Chicago: Follett, 1970. 256p.

National Directory for the Performing Arts and Civic Centers.
Dallas: Handel and Co. , 1973. 604p.

Noll, Roger G. ; Merton J. Peck, and John J. McGowan.
Economic Aspects of Television Regulation. Washington,
D. C. : Brookings Institution, 1973. 342p.

Parker, Ben R. , and Pat J. Drabik. Creative Intention.
New York: Law-Arts, 1972.

Peck, William Allen. Anatomy of Local Radio-TV Copy. 3d
ed. Blue Ridge Summit, Pa. : G/L Tab Books, 1968. 93p.

Peck, William Allen. Radio Promotion Handbook. Blue Ridge
Summit, Pa. : G/L Tab Books, 1968. 191p.

Peterson, Theodore Bernard, and Jay W. Jensen. The Mass
Media and Modern Society. New York: Holt, Rinehart
& Winston, 1965. 259p.

Phillips, Gene D. The Movie Makers: Artists in an Industry. Chicago: Nelson-Hall, 1973. 249p.

Phillips, Mary Alice Mayer. CATV: A History of Community Antenna Television. Evanston, Ill. : Northwestern
University Press, 1972. 209p.

Powers, Ron. The Newscasters: The News Business as
Show Business. New York: St. Martin's Press, 1977.
243p.

Price, Monroe E. , and John Wickleim. Cable Television:
A Guide for Citizen Action. Foreword by Everett C.
Parker. Philadelphia: Pilgrim Press, 1972. 160p.

Quaal, Ward L., and James A. Brown. Broadcast Management: Radio and Television. 2d ed. New York: Hastings House, 1976. 464p.

Quigley, Martin, and Richard Gertner. Films in America, 1929-1969. New York: Golden, 1970. 379p.

Randall, Richard S. Censorship of the Movies; The Social and Political Control of a Mass Medium. Madison: University of Wisconsin Press, 1968. 280p.

Rissover, Fredric, and David C. Birch. Mass Media and the Popular Arts. New York: McGraw-Hill, 1971. 348p.

Rivkin, Steven R. Cable Television: A Guide to Federal Regulations. New York: Crane, Russak, 1974. 390p.

Routt, Edd. The Business of Radio Broadcasting. Blue Ridge Summit, Pa.: G/L Tab Books, 1972. 400p.

Sadoul, Georges. Dictionary of Film Makers. Translated, edited and updated by Peter Morris. Berkeley: University of California Press, 1972. 288p.

Sadoul Georges. Dictionary of Films. Translated, edited and updated by Peter Morris. Berkeley: University of California Press, 1972. 432p.

Schiller, Herbert I. The Mind Managers. Boston: Beacon Press, 1973. 214p.

Screen Actors Guild. The Story of the Screen Actors Guild. Hollywood, Calif.: Public Relations Department, Screen Actors Guild, 1966. 23p.

Seiden, Martin H. Who Controls the Mass Media? Popular Myths and Economic Realities. New York: Basic Books, 1974. 246p.

Shemel, Sidney, and M. William Krasilovsky. This Business of Music. Rev. and enl. Copyright Act ed. Edited by Paul Ackerman. New York: Billboard, 1977. 575p.

Sitney, P. Adams, editor. Film Culture Reader. New York: Praeger, 1970. 438p.

Skornia, Harry Jay, comp. Problems and Controversies in Television and Radio. Basic readings selected and edited by Harry J. Skornia and Jack William Kitson. Palo Alto, Calif.: Pacific Books, 1968. 503p.

Smith, David R. "Jack Benny Checklist: Radio, Television, Motion Pictures, Books and Articles." Los Angeles: University of California Library, 1970. 33p.

Statistical Research, Inc. "A Study of the Consistency of Local Market Television Ratings." Westfield, N. J., 1970.

Statistical Trends in Broadcasting. 10th ed. New York: Blair Television/Blair Radio Divisions of John Blair and Co., 1974. 53p.

Steinberg, Charles S. The Communicative Arts: An Introduction to Mass Media. New York: Hastings House, 1970. 371p.

Steinberg, Charles S. Mass Media and Communication. 2d rev. ed. New York: Hastings House, 1972. 686p.

Stormes, John M., and James P. Crumpler. Television Communications Systems for Business and Industry. New York: Wiley-Interscience, 1970. 238p.

Sweeney, Russell C. Coming Next Week: A Pictorial History of Film Advertising. South Brunswick, N. J.: A. S. Barnes, 1973. 303p.

Truitt, Evelyn Mack. Who Was Who on Screen. New York: Bowker, 1974. 363p.

Tyrrell, R. W. The Work of the Television Journalist. London: Focal Press, 1972. 176p.

Variety. Weekly. Syd Silverman, editor. Variety, Inc., 154 W. 46th St., New York, N. Y. 10036. Advertising; film, music, play, radio, record, and television reviews.

Video Resources in New York State. Prepared by the Film and Video Bureau with support from the New York State Council on the Arts. New York: Publishing Center for Cultural Resources, 1975. 64p.

Wainwright, Charles Anthony. Television Commercials; How

to Create Successful TV Advertising. Rev. ed. New York: Hastings House, 1970. 318p.

Wells, Alan. Mass Media and Society. Palo Alto, Calif. : National Press Books, 1972. 407p.

Westmore, Frank, and Muriel Davidson. The Westmores of Hollywood. New York: Lippincott, 1976. 256p.

IX

MUSEUM MANAGEMENT AND THE ARTS

American Association of Museums. America's Museums; The Belmont Report. Washington, D. C. , 1968. 81p.

American Association of Museums. Museum Training Courses in the United States and Canada. Rev. ed. Washington, D. C. , 1971. 51p.

American Association of Museums. Museums: Their New Audience. Washington, D. C. : American Association of Museums, 1972. 112p.

American Association of Museums. 1971 Financial and Salary Survey. Washington, D. C. , 1971. 92p.

American Association of Museums. A Statistical Survey of Museums in the United States and Canada. Washington, D. C. , 1965. 52p.

Art Works: Law, Policy, Practice. Edited by Franklin Feldman and Stephen E. Weil. New York: Practising Law Institute, 1974. 1241p.

Association of Art Museum Directors. Professional Practices Committee. Professional Practices in Art Museums; Report. New York, 1971. 28p.

Burnham, Sophy. The Art Crowd. New York: McKay, 1973. 395p.

Burt, Nathaniel. Palaces for the People: A Social History of the American Art Museum. Boston: Little, Brown, 1977. 446p.

Canfield, Cass. The Incredible Pierpont Morgan: Financier and Art Collector. New York: Harper & Row, 1974. 176p.

54

Chenhall, Robert G. Museum Cataloging in the Computer Age. Nashville, Tenn.: American Association for State and Local History, 1975. 261p.

Computers and Their Potential Applications in Museums; A Conference Sponsored by the Metropolitan Museum of Art, April 15, 16, 17, 1968. New York: Arno Press, 1968. 402p.

Dudley, Dorothy H.; Irma Bezold Wilkinson, and others. Museum Registration Methods. Rev. ed. Washington, D. C.: American Association of Museums, 1968. 294p.

Educational Facilities Laboratories. The Arts in Found Places. A Report from EFL and the National Endowment for the Arts. New York, 1976. 138p.

Educational Facilities Laboratories. Hands-On Museums: Partners in Learning. New York, 1975. 44p.

Educational Facilities Laboratories. New Places for the Arts: A Report from EFL and the National Endowment for the Arts. New York, 1976. 75p.

Gladstone, M. J. A Report on Professional Salaries in New York State Museums. New York: New York State Association of Museums, 1972. 47p.

Handbook of Museums: Germany, Austria, Switzerland. (Handbuch der Museen: Deutschland BRD, DDR, Österreich, Schweiz.) Munich: Verlag Dokumentation, 1971. 2 volumes, 1300p. (Distributed in Western Hemisphere by R. R. Bowker.)

Hess, John L. The Grand Acquisitors. Boston: Houghton Mifflin, 1974. 178p.

Hudson, Kenneth, and Ann Nicholls, editors. Directory of World Museums. New York: Columbia University Press, 1975. 864p.

Keck, Caroline. A Handbook on the Care of Paintings, for Historical Agencies and Small Museums. Nashville, Tenn.: American Association for State and Local History, 1965. 132p.

Kort, Michele F. White-Collar Unions in Art Museums: The

Collective Response. Los Angeles: Graduate School of Management, University of California, 1974. 85p. (Comprehensive research paper for UCLA Management in the Arts Program.)

Lerman, Leo. The Museum: One Hundred Years and the Metropolitan Museum of Art. Introduction by Thomas P. F. Hoving. New York: Viking, 1969. 400p.

Levy, Howard, and Lynn Ross-Molloy. Beginning a Community Museum. New York: New York Foundation for the Arts, 1975. 85p.

Lewis, Ralph H. Manual for Museums. Washington, D. C.: National Park Service, U. S. Department of the Interior, 1976. 412p.

Libraries, Museums and Art Galleries Yearbook. Irregular. New York: Bowker.

Los Angeles County, California. County Museum of Art. A Report on the Art and Technology Program of the Los Angeles County Museum of Art, 1967-1971. Introduction by Maurice Tuchman. Los Angeles, 1971.

McWhinney, William H., and James M. Woods. "A Curator for the Future." Los Angeles: Graduate School of Management, University of California, 1972. 11p. (Management in the Arts Research Paper No. 18.)

Mandl, Cynthia K., and Robert M. Kerr. Museum Sponsorship of Performing Arts. Madison: Center for Arts Administration, Graduate School of Business, University of Wisconsin, 1975. 45p.

A Museum for the People; A Report of Proceedings at the Seminar on Neighborhood Museums, Held November 20, 21, and 22, 1969, at MUSE, the Bedford Lincoln Neighborhood Museum in Brooklyn, New York. Edited by Emily Dennis Harvey and Bernard J. Friedberg. New York: Arno Press, 1971. 86p.

Museums of the World. Museen der Welt. Munich: Verlag Dokumentation, 1973. 762p.

National Council of YMCA's. Training Volunteer Leaders. Fairfax, Va.: NTL Learning Resources Corp., 1974. 189p.

National Endowment for the Arts. Museums, U. S. A. : Art, History, Science, and Others. Washington, D. C. : U. S. Government Printing Office, 1974. 203p.

National Research Center of the Arts. Museums, U. S. A. : A Survey Report. Washington, D. C. : National Endowment for the Arts, 1975. 592p.

O'Doherty, Brian. Museums in Crisis. With a foreword by Nancy Hanks. New York: George Braziller, 1972. 178p.

The Official Museum Directory: United States, Canada. Biennial. Washington, D. C. : American Association of Museums.

On Understanding Art Museums. Englewood Cliffs, N. J. : Prentice-Hall, 1975. 212p.

Rogers, Lola Eriksen. Museums and Related Institutions; A Basic Program Survey. Prepared by the U. S. Office of Education, Washington, D. C. : U. S. Government Printing Office, 1969. 120p.

Schwalbe, Douglas, and Janet Baker-Carr. Conflict in the Arts: The Relocation of Authority. Volume 3, The Museum. Cambridge, Mass. : Arts Administration Research Institute, 1976. 82p.

Spaeth, Eloise. American Art Museums: An Introduction to Looking. 3d ed. , expanded. New York: Harper & Row, 1975. 483p.

Tamarind Lithography Workshop. Acquiring an Inventory of Original Prints--An Art Market Study. Prepared by Calvin J. Goodman. Los Angeles, 1969. 53p.

Tamarind Lithography Workshop. Business Methods for a Lithography Workshop. Prepared by Calvin J. Goodman. Los Angeles, 1967. 240p.

Tamarind Lithography Workshop. "Gallery Facility Planning for Marketing Original Prints. " Los Angeles, 1967. 36p.

Tamarind Lithography Workshop. "How a Lithograph Is Made-- and How Much It Costs. " Los Angeles, 1966. 18p.

58 / The Arts and Business

Tamarind Lithography Workshop. A Management Study of an
    Art Gallery; Its Structure, Sales and Personnel. Los
    Angeles, 1966. 110p.

Tamarind Lithography Workshop. Sex Differentials in Art Ex-
    hibition Reviews: A Statistical Study. Los Angeles,
    1972. 132p.

Tamarind Lithography Workshop. A Study of the Marketing
    of the Original Print. Prepared by Calvin J. Goodman.
    Los Angeles, 1964. 94p. (Based on A Study of the
    Marketing of Fine Prints to Serve Contemporary Ameri-
    can Artists.)

Tomkins, Calvin. Merchants and Masterpieces: The Story
    of the Metropolitan Museum of Art. New York: E. P.
    Dutton, 1970. 383p.

Walker, John. Self-Portrait with Donors: Confessions of an
    Art Collector. Boston: Little, Brown, 1974. 320p.

Wasserman, Paul, and Esther Herman, editors. Museum
    Media; A Biennial Directory and Index of Publications
    and Audiovisuals Available from United States and Cana-
    dian Institutions. Detroit: Gale Research Company.

Wittlin, Alma S. Museums: In Search of a Usable Future.
    Cambridge, Mass.: M. I. T. Press, 1970. 299p.

X

MUSIC

Adizes, Ichak. Seattle Opera Association; A Policy Making Case for Management in the Arts. Los Angeles: Graduate School of Management, University of California, 1971. 53p. (Management in the Arts Research Paper no. 5.)

Arian, Edward. Bach, Beethoven, and Bureaucracy: The Case of the Philadelphia Orchestra. University: University of Alabama Press, 1971. 158p.

Arts Council of Great Britain. A Report on Orchestral Resources in Great Britain, 1970. London, 1970. 125p.

Berk, Lee Eliot. Legal Protection for the Creative Musician. Boston: Berklee Press, 1970. 371p.

Blaine, Martha. "The Parkview Symphony: Cases A and B. " Los Angeles: Graduate School of Management, University of California, 1971. 20p. (Management in the Arts Research Paper no. 10.)

British Music Yearbook. Annual. Edited by Arthur Jacobs. Ann Arbor, Mich. : Bowker.

Davis, Clive, with James Willwerth. Clive: Inside the Record Business. New York: Morrow, 1974. 300p.

Eaton, Quaintance. Opera Production II: A Handbook. Minneapolis: University of Minnesota Press, 1974. 347p.

Federal Bar Association of New York, New Jersey and Connecticut. Committee on the Law of the Theatre. The Business and Law of Music; A Symposium. Edited by Joseph Taubman. New York: Federal Legal Publications, 1965. 111p.

Ford Foundation. Finances of the Performing Arts. Volume
  I, A Survey of 166 Professional Nonprofit Resident
  Theaters, Operas, Symphonies, Ballets, and Modern
  Dance Companies. Volume II, A Survey of the Characteristics and Attitudes of Audiences for Theater, Opera, Symphony and Ballet in 12 U.S. Cities. New York,
  1974. 2 volumes.

Garrison, Lee C., and Christina Vogl Kaali-Nagy. "Comparative Profiles of Users and Nonusers of the Los Angeles
  Music Center." Los Angeles: Graduate School of Management, University of California, 1971. 38p. (Management in the Arts Research Paper No. 13.)

Hart, Philip. Orpheus in the New World: The Symphony
  Orchestra as an American Cultural Institution. New
  York: Norton, 1973. 562p.

Huntley, Leston. The Language of the Music Business; A
  Handbook of Its Customs, Practices and Procedures.
  Nashville, Tenn.: Del Capo Publications, 1965. 465p.

International Music Industry Conference, 1st, Paradise Island,
  Nassau, 1969. The Complete Report of the First Inter-
  national Music Industry Conference. Edited by Paul
  Ackerman and Lee Zhito. New York: Billboard Pub.
  Co., 1969. 335p.

Kaplan, Benjamin, and Ralph S. Brown, Jr. Cases on Copyright, Unfair Competition, and Other Topics Bearing on
  the Protection of Literary, Musical, and Artistic Works.
  2d ed. Mineola, N.Y.: Foundation Press, 1974. 997p.

Karshner, Roger. The Music Machine. Los Angeles: Nash
  Pub. Co., 1971. 196p.

Krawitz, Herman E., with Howard K. Klein. Royal American
  Symphonic Theater: A Radical Proposal for a Subsidized
  Professional Theater. New York: Macmillan, 1975.
  211p.

Legal and Business Problems of the Record Industry. Donald
  E. Biederman, chairman. New York: Practising Law
  Institute, 1974. 536p.

Leinsdorf, Erich. Cadenza: A Musical Career. Boston:
  Houghton Mifflin, 1976. 321p.

Mueller, Kate Hevner. Twenty-Seven Major American Symphony Orchestras: A History and Analysis of Their Repertoires Seasons 1942-43 Through 1969-70. Bloomington: Indiana University Press, 1974. 464p.

Murphy, Judith, and George Sullivan. Music in American Society; An Interpretive Report of the Tanglewood Symposium. Washington, D. C.: Music Educators National Conference, 1968. 72p.

The Music Educator's Business Handbook. Washington, D. C.: Music Industry Council, 1970.

The Musician's Guide. New York: Music Information Service, 1972. 1014p.

Nimmer, Melville B. Nimmer on Copyright; A Treatise on the Law of Literary, Musical and Artistic Property, and the Protection of Ideas. Albany, N. Y.: Mathew Bender, 1963- . Looseleaf.

Pauly, Reinhard G. Music and the Theatre: An Introduction to Opera. Englewood Cliffs, N. J.: Prentice-Hall, 1970. 462p.

Pavlakis, Christopher. The American Music Handbook. New York: Free Press, 1974. 836p.

Roth, Ernst. The Business of Music; Reflections of a Music Publisher. New York: Oxford University Press, 1969. 269p.

Salem, Mahmoud. Organizational Survival in the Performing Arts: The Making of the Seattle Opera. New York: Praeger, 1976. 210p.

Schlesinger, Janet. Challenge to the Urban Orchestra; The Case of the Pittsburgh Symphony. Released through Eastern Gas and Fuel Associates, 1971. 163p. (Available from Wallingford Group, Ltd., 4766 Wallingford St., Pittsburgh, Pa. 15213.)

Schwalbe, Douglas, and Janet Baker-Carr. Conflict in the Arts: The Relocation of Authority. Volume 2, The Orchestra. Cambridge, Mass.: Arts Administration Research Institute, 1977. 68p.

Seltzer, George. The Professional Symphony Orchestra in the United States. Metuchen, N. J. : Scarecrow Press, 1975. 486p.

Shemel, Sidney, and M. William Krasilovsky. This Business of Music. Rev. & enl. Copyright Act ed. Edited by Paul Ackerman. New York: Billboard, 1977. 575p.

Spiegel, Irwin O. , and Jay L. Cooper, compilers and editors. Record and Music Publishing Forms of Agreement in Current. New York: Law-Arts, 1971. Looseleaf.

Swoboda, Henry, compiler. The American Symphony Orchestra. New York: Basic Books, 1967. 208p.

Variety. Weekly. Syd Silverman, editor. Variety, Inc. , 154 W. 46th St. , New York, N. Y. 10036. Advertising; film, music, play, radio, record, and television reviews.

Wechsberg, Joseph. The Opera. New York: Macmillan, 1972. 312p.

Young, Jean, and Jim Young. Succeeding in the Big World of Music. Boston: Little, Brown, 1977. 306p.

XI

NOVELS, BIOGRAPHIES, HISTORIES

Adams, Laurie. Art Cop, Robert Volpe: Art Crime Detective. New York: Dodd, Mead, 1974. 240p.

Archer, Jeffrey. Not a Penny More, Not a Penny Less. New York: Doubleday, 1976.

Arleo, Joseph. Home Late. New York: Warner, 1974.

Balio, Tino. United Artists: The Company Built By the Stars. Madison: University of Wisconsin Press, 1976. 323p.

Brodeur, Paul. The Stunt Man. New York: Atheneum, 1970. 278p.

Broun, Daniel. The Production; A Novel of the Broadway Theater. New York: Dial, 1970. 369p.

Canfield, Cass. The Incredible Pierpont Morgan: Financier and Art Collector. New York: Harper & Row, 1974. 176p.

Carter, Robert A. Manhattan Primitive. New York: Stein & Day, 1971. 249p.

Charles, Gerda. The Destiny Waltz. New York: Scribner's, 1971. 429p.

Churchill, Allen. The Splendor Seekers: An Informal Glimpse of America's Multimillionaire Spenders--Members of the $50,000,000 Club. New York: Grosset & Dunlap, 1974. 278p.

Connell, Evan S. The Connoisseur. New York: Knopf, 1974. 197p.

Creasey, John. Gideon's Art. By J. J. Marric. New York:
Harper and Row, 1971. 217p.

Davis, Christopher. The Producer. (An "autobiography.")
New York: Harper and Row, 1972. 321p.

Dennis, Patrick. How Firm a Foundation. New York: Pocket Books, 1969, c1968. 248p.

Eames, John Douglas. The MGM Story: The Complete History of Fifty Roaring Years. New York: Crown Publishers, 1975. 400p.

Easton, Carol. The Search for Sam Goldwyn. New York:
Morrow, 1976. 304p.

Friedman, Bernard Harper. Museum: A Novel. New York:
Fiction Collective, 1974. 156p.

Gerson, Noel B. Jefferson Square. New York: M. Evans,
1968. 503p. (distributed in association with Lippincott.)

Gerson, Noel B. Talk Show. New York: Morrow, 1971.
320p.

Goldman, James. The Man from Greek and Roman. New
York: Random House, 1974. 251p.

Goldsmith, Barbara. The Straw Man. New York: Farrar,
Straus & Giroux, 1975. 263p.

Greenfield, Jeff. Television: The First Fifty Years. New
York: Abrams, 1977. 320p.

Higham, Charles. Warner Brothers. New York: Scribner's,
1975. 232p.

Hochman, Sandra. Happiness Is Too Much Trouble. New
York: Putnam, 1976. 256p.

Irving, Clifford. Fake: The Story of Elmyr de Hory, the
Greatest Art Forger of Our Time. (A "biography.")
New York: McGraw-Hill, 1969. 243p.

Jesmer, Elaine. Number One: With a Bullet. New York:
Farrar, Straus & Giroux, 1974. 423p.

Lawton, Richard. Grand Illusions. Text by Hugo Leckey. London: Octopus Books, 1974. 255p.

Lawton, Richard. A World of Movies: 70 Years of Film History. London: Octopus Books, 1974. 383p.

Leinsdorf, Erich. Cadenza: A Musical Career. Boston: Houghton Mifflin, 1976. 321p.

Levine, Faye. The Culture Barons. New York: T. Y. Crowell, 1976. 312p.

Levy, Julien. Memoir of an Art Gallery. New York: Putnam, 1977. 320p.

Lyons, Timothy James. The Silent Partner: The History of the American Film Manufacturing Company, 1910-1921. New York: Arno Press, 1974. 256p.

Marks, Peter. Collector's Choice. New York: Random House, 1972. 211p.

Marx, Arthur. Goldwyn: A Biography of the Man Behind the Myth. New York: Norton, 1976. 376p.

Marx, Samuel. Mayer and Thalberg: The Make-Believe Saints. New York: Random House, 1975. 273p.

Method to the Madness (Hollywood Explained). Edited by Dick Atkins and a cast of six. Livingston, N. J. : Prince Publishers, 1975. 207p.

Metz, Robert. CBS: Reflections in a Bloodshot Eye. Chicago: Playboy Press, 1975. 428p.

O'Neal, Cothburn. The Money Hunters: A Behind-the-Scenes Novel of Professional Fund-Raisers. New York: Crown, 1966. 218p.

Powers, Ron. The Newscasters: The News Business as Show Business. New York: St. Martin's Press, 1977. 243p.

Prior, Allan. The Contract. New York: Simon & Schuster, 1971. 376p.

Purtell, Joseph. The Tiffany Touch. New York: Random House, 1971. 309p.

Rotsler, William. Patron of the Arts. New York: Ballantine, 1974. 210p.

Russcol, Herbert, and Margalit Banai. Philharmonic. New York: Coward, McCann & Geoghegan, 1971. 298p.

Selcamm, George. Fifty-Seventh Street. New York: Norton, 1971. 344p.

Stern, Daniel. Final Cut. New York: Viking Press, 1975. 279p.

Truitt, Evelyn Mack. Who Was Who on Screen. New York: Bowker, 1974. 363p.

Walker, John. Self-Portrait with Donors: Confessions of an Art Collector. Boston: Little, Brown, 1974. 320p.

Westmore, Frank, and Muriel Davidson. The Westmores of Hollywood. New York: Lippincott, 1976. 256p.

XII

THE PERFORMING ARTS

ACUCAA Handbook: Presenting the Performing Arts. Madison,
    Wis. : Association of College, University and Community
    Arts Administrators, 1977. Looseleaf.

Adizes, Ichak. The Seattle Opera Association: A Policy
    Making Case for Management in the Arts. Los Angeles:
    Graduate School of Management, University of California,
    1971. 53p. (Management in the Arts Research Paper no.
    5.) (Available as # 9-371-679 through Intercollegiate
    Case Clearing House, Soldiers Field Post Office, Bos-
    ton, Mass. 02163.)

Adizes, Ichak. "The Unique Character of Performing Arts
    Organizations and the Functioning of Their Boards of
    Directors (A Managerial Analysis). " Los Angeles:
    Graduate School of Management, University of California,
    1971. 14p. (Management in the Arts Research Paper
    no. 4.)

Arts Council of Great Britain. A Report on Opera and Ballet
    in the United Kingdom, 1966-69. London, 1969. 80p.

Association of College and University Concert Managers.
    ACUCM Workbook; A Guide to Presenting the Perform-
    ing Arts on College and University Campuses. Prepared
    by Fannie Taylor. Madison, Wis. : Association of Col-
    lege and University Concert Managers, 1968. 117p.

Baumol, William J. , and William G. Bowen. Performing
    Arts, the Economic Dilemma; A Study of Problems Com-
    mon to Theater, Opera, Music and Dance. New York:
    Twentieth Century Fund, 1966. 582p.

Beverly Hills Bar Association. Program on Legal Aspects

of the Entertainment Industry. (See entry under Part
VI, Legal Aspects of the Arts.)

California. Arts Commission. The California Dance Directory. Presented by the California Arts Commission and
the Association of American Dance Companies. Sacramento, 1972. 78p.

Center Theatre Group. Box Office Guidelines. New York:
Foundation for the Extension and Development of the
American Professional Theatre, 1974. 44p.

Cohen, Selma Jeanne. Dance as a Theatre Art: Source
Readings in Dance History from 1581 to the Present.
New York: Dodd, Mead, 1974. 224p.

Community Support of the Performing Arts; Selected Problems
of Local and National Interest. Edited by Allan Easton.
Hempstead, N.Y.: Hofstra University, 1970. 327p.
(Hofstra University Yearbook of Business, series 7,
1970, v. 5.)

Cultural Post. Irregularly published, 1-2 issues per year.
National Endowment for the Arts, Washington, D.C.,
20506. Bibliographies, illustrations. Tabloid format.

Dace, Wallace. Subsidies for the Theater; A Study of the
Central European System of Financing Drama, Opera
and Ballet, 1968-1970. Manhattan, Kan.: AG Press,
1972. 188p.

Eaton, Quaintance. Opera Production II: A Handbook. Minneapolis: University of Minnesota Press, 1974. 347p.

Ford Foundation. Finances of the Performing Arts. Volume
I, A Survey of 166 Professional Nonprofit Resident
Theaters, Operas, Symphonies, Ballets, and Modern
Dance Companies. Volume II, A Survey of the Charac-
teristics and Attitudes of Audiences for Theater, Opera,
Symphony, and Ballet in 12 U.S. Cities. New York,
1974. 2 volumes.

Granfield, Michael. "The Live Performing Arts: Financial
Catastrophe or Economic Catharsis?" Los Angeles:
Graduate School of Management, University of California,
1971. 23p. (Management in the Arts Research Paper
no. 8.)

Henry, Austin H. , and E. Arthur Prieve. "Improved Financial Management of Smaller Performing Arts Organizations. " Madison: Center for Arts Administration, Graduate School of Business, University of Wisconsin, 1973.
36p.

Kaderlan, Norman S. The Role of the Arts Administrator.
Madison: Center for Arts Administration, Graduate
School of Business, University of Wisconsin, 1973. 47p.

Kraus, Richard G. History of the Dance in Art and Education. Englewood Cliffs, N. J. : Prentice-Hall, 1969.
371p.

Los Angeles Dance Theatre. Grant Program [of the] Los An-
geles Dance Theatre [and] American School of Dance.
Hollywood, Calif. : Los Angeles Dance Theatre, 1970.
Unpaged.

Mandl, Cynthia K. , and Robert M. Kerr. Museum Sponsorship of Performing Arts. Madison: Center for Arts
Administration, Graduate School of Business, University
of Wisconsin, 1975. 45p.

Mann, Peter H. The Provincial Audience for Drama, Ballet
and Opera; A Survey in Leeds; A Report to the Arts
Council of Great Britain. Leeds: Department of So-
ciological Studies, University of Sheffield, 1969. 80p.

Martin, Ralph G. Lincoln Center for the Performing Arts.
Englewood Cliffs, N. J. : Prentice-Hall, 1971. 192p.

Moskow, Michael H. Labor Relations in the Performing
Arts; An Introductory Survey. Foreword by John T.
Dunlop. New York: Associated Councils of the Arts,
1969. 218p.

National Directory for the Performing Arts and Civic Centers.
Edited by Beatrice Handel, Janet Spencer and Nolanda
Turner. Dallas: Handel, 1975. 972p.

National Directory for the Performing Arts/Educational.
Edited by Beatrice Handel, Nolanda Turner and Janet
Spencer. Dallas: Handel, 1975. 821p.

National Endowment for the Arts. "Economic Aspects of the
Performing Arts--A Portrait in Figures. " Washington,
D. C. : U. S. Government Printing Office, 1971. 23p.

National Research Center of the Arts. The Public Service Budget of Arts and Cultural Organizations: A Better Measure of Full Financial Need. New York: Associated Councils of the Arts, 1977. 104p.

Nimmer, Melville B. Nimmer on Copyright; A Treatise on the Law of Literary, Musical and Artistic Property, and the Protection of Ideas. Albany, N. Y.: Mathew Bender, 1963- . Looseleaf.

Pacific Northwest Ballet Association. Advisory Seminar Held June 25, 1972, Seattle, Washington, for the Council of Dance Educators, a Community Action Branch of the Pacific Northwest Ballet Association. Seattle, 1972. 83p.

Pauly, Reinhard G. Music and the Theater; An Introduction to Opera. Englewood Cliffs, N. J.: Prentice-Hall, 1970. 462p.

Performing Arts in Asia. Edited and with introductions by James R. Brandon. Paris: UNESCO, 1971. 168p.

Poggi, Jack. Theater in America: The Impact of Economic Forces, 1870-1967. Ithaca, N. Y.: Cornell University Press, 1968. 328p.

Pride, Leo Bryan. International Theatre Directory; A World Directory of the Theatre and Performing Arts. New York: Simon & Schuster, 1973. 577p.

Prince, Harold S. Contradictions: Notes on Twenty-Six Years in the Theatre. New York: Dodd, Mead, 1974. 242p.

Reische, Diana L. The Performing Arts in America. New York: H. W. Wilson, 1973. 252p.

Rockefeller Brothers Fund. The Performing Arts: Problems and Prospects; Rockefeller Panel Report on the Future of Theatre, Dance, Music in America. New York: McGraw-Hill, 1965. 258p.

Salem, Mahmoud. Organizational Survival in the Performing Arts: The Making of the Seattle Opera. New York: Praeger, 1976. 210p.

Schoolcraft, Ralph Newman. Performing Arts/Books in Print: An Annotated Bibliography. New York: Drama Book Specialists, 1973. 761p.

Schubart, Mark. Performing Arts Institutions and Young People; Lincoln Center's Study: "The Hunting of the Squiggle." New York: Praeger, 1972. 108p.

Seltzer, George. The Professional Symphony Orchestra in the United States. Metuchen, N.J.: Scarecrow Press, 1975. 486p.

Stern, Lawrence. Stage Management: A Guidebook of Practical Techniques. Boston: Allyn & Bacon, 1974. 323p.

TCG Fiscal Survey. Annual. Prepared by James Copeland, program director. New York: Theatre Communications Group.

Taubman, Joseph. Performing Arts Management and Law. New York: Law-Arts Publishers, 1972. 4 volumes.

Theatre Profiles: An Informational Handbook of Nonprofit Professional Theatres in the United States. Bi-annual. Editor: Lindy Zesch, with Marsue Cumming. New York: Theatre Communications Group.

Touring Directory of the Performing Arts in Canada. Ottawa: Information Canada, 1975.

Truitt, Evelyn Mack. Who Was Who on Screen. New York: Bowker, 1974. 363p.

Twentieth Century Fund. Task Force on Performing Arts Centers. Bricks, Mortar and the Performing Arts; Report. Background paper by Martin Mayer. New York, 1970. 99p.

Variety. Weekly. Syd Silverman, editor. Variety, Inc., 154 W. 46th St., New York, N.Y. 10036. Advertising; film, music, play, radio, record, and television reviews.

Voegeli, Thomas J. Handbook for Tour Management. Madison Center for Arts Administration, Graduate School of Business, University of Wisconsin, 1975. 55p.

Vogt, Marie. The Businessman's Ballet Book. Sylvania, Ohio, 1973. 50p.

Wechsberg, Joseph. The Opera. New York: Macmillan, 1972. 312p.

Wehle, Mary M. Financial Practice for Performing Arts Companies--A Manual. Cambridge, Mass. : Arts Administration Research Institute, 1977. 154p.

Westmore, Frank, and Muriel Davidson. The Westmores of Hollywood. New York: Lippincott, 1976. 256p.

Whalon, Marion K. Performing Arts Research: A Guide to Information Sources. Detroit: Gale Research, 1976. 280p.

XIII

SOCIETY AND THE ARTS

Ad Hoc Coalition of States for the Arts in Education. Comprehensive Arts Planning. New York: coordinated by the JDR 3rd Fund, 1975. 111p.

Adizes, Ichak, and William McWhinney. "Arts, Society and Administration: The Role and Training of Arts Administrators. " Los Angeles: Graduate School of Management, University of California, 1971. 16p. (Management in the Arts Research Paper no. 9.)

American Council for the Arts in Education. Community Arts and Community Survival; An Event in Los Angeles, June 1972. By Judith Murphy. Cosponsored by the Los Angeles Community Arts Alliance and the Department of Arts and Humanities, University Extension, University of California, Los Angeles. (The Eleventh Annual Conference of the American Council for the Arts in Education.) New York, 1973. 130p.

"Americans and the Arts; Highlights from a Survey of Public Opinion. " New York: Associated Councils of the Arts, 1974. 36p.

Arey, June Batten. State Arts Agencies in Transition: Purpose, Program, and Personnel. Wayzata, Minn. : Spring Hill Conference Center, 1975. 267p.

Art and Sexual Politics; Women's Liberation, Women Artists, and Art History. Edited by Thomas B. Hess and Elizabeth C. Baker. New York: Macmillan, 1973. 150p.

The Arts and Man; A World View of the Role and Function of the Arts in Society. Englewood Cliffs, N. J. : Prentice-Hall, 1969. 171p.

The Arts and the Public. Essays by Saul Bellow and others. Edited by James E. Miller and Paul D. Herring. Chicago: University of Chicago Press, 1967. 266p.

The Arts at the Grass Roots. Edited by Bruce Cutler. Lawrence: University of Kansas Press, 1968. 270p.

Arts Council of Great Britain. Annual Report. London.

Arts Councils of America. The Arts: A Central Element of a Good Society; Eleventh National Conference, June 16-19, 1965, Washington, D. C. New York, 1966. 145p.

Arts in Society. Ceased publication with v. 13, no. 2, Summer-Fall 1976; formerly issued 3 times yearly. Edward L. Kamarck, editor. Extension. University of Wisconsin. Advertising, book reviews, illustrations, index. Circulation was 5000. The following issues are recommended:

> The Arts and the Black Revolution--I, v. 1, no. 2, Summer-Fall 1968.
> The Arts and the Black Revolution--II, v. 5, no. 3, Fall-Winter 1968.
> The Arts and the Human Environment, v. 8, no. 2, Summer-Fall 1971.
> The Social Uses of Art, v. 9, no. 3, Fall-Winter 1972.
> Women and the Arts, v. 11, no. 1, Spring-Summer 1974.

Associated Councils of the Arts. The Arts: Planning for Change; Proceedings of the Twelfth National Conference, Associated Councils of the Arts, Formerly Arts Councils of America, May 19-21, 1966, New York. New York, 1966. 131p.

Associated Councils of the Arts. A Guide to Community Arts Agencies. Edited by Michael K. Newton and Barbara B. Israel. New York, 1974. 373p.

Baynes, Ken. Art in Society. Woodstock, N. Y.: Overlook Press, 1975. 288p.

Bell, Daniel. The Cultural Contradictions of Capitalism. New York: Basic Books, 1976. 301p.

Bullock, Paul. Creative Careers: Minorities in the Arts. Los Angeles: Institute of Industrial Relations, University of California, 1977. 220p.

Burnham, Bennie. The Art Crisis. New York: St. Martin's Press, 1975. 256p.

Burns, Joan Simpson. The Awkward Embrace: The Creative Artist and the Institution in America. New York: Knopf, 1975. 512p.

Center for the Study of Democratic Institutions. "The Arts in a Democratic Society." By Gifford Phillips, including a discussion with Roger L. Stevens and others on the new program of federal aid for the arts. Santa Barbara, Calif.: Center for the Study of Democratic Institutions, 1966. 35p.

Churchill, Allen. The Splendor Seekers: An Informal Glimpse of America's Multimillionaire Spenders--Members of the $50,000,000 Club. New York: Grosset & Dunlap, 1974. 278p.

Community Support of the Performing Arts; Selected Problems of Local and National Interest. Edited by Allan Easton. Hempstead, N.Y.: Hofstra University, 1970. 327p. Hofstra University Yearbook of Business, series 7, 1970, v. 5.

Corson, John Jay. Business in the Humane Society. New York: McGraw-Hill, 1971. 314p.

Cultural Post. Irregularly published, 1-2 issues per year. Washington, D.C.: National Endowment for the Arts. Bibliographies, illustrations. Tabloid format.

Cwi, David. In Search of a Regional Policy for the Arts. Baltimore: Joint Committee on Cultural Resources, 1975. 186p.

Davis, Douglas M. Art and the Future; A History/Prophecy of the Collaboration Between Science, Technology, and Art. New York: Praeger, 1973. 208p.

Davis, Keith. Business and Society: Environment and Responsibility. 3d ed. New York: McGraw-Hill, 1975. 597p.

Educational Facilities Laboratories. Arts and the Handicapped: An Issue of Access. A Report from Educational Facilities Laboratories and the National Endowment for the Arts. New York, 1975. 78p.

Fort Wayne Fine Arts Foundation. "A Proposal to Establish a Community Arts School." Prepared by the Concerned Citizens of Fort Wayne, Ind. Fort Wayne, 1972. 32p.

Gans, Herbert J. Popular Culture and High Culture. New York: Basic Books, 1974. 179p.

Gardner, Howard. The Arts and Human Development; A Psychological Study of the Artistic Process. New York: Wiley, 1973. 395p.

Goodman, Richard, and Mirta Samuelson. "An Exploration into the Administrative Support of the Creative Process: The Theater Case." Los Angeles: Graduate School of Management, University of California, 1970. 13p. (Management in the Arts Research Paper no. 6.)

Human Resources Network. The Handbook of Corporate Social Responsibility: Profiles of Involvement. 2d ed. Radnor, Pa.: Chilton Book Co., 1975. 629p.

Johnson, Alton C., and E. Arthur Prieve. Older Americans: The Unrealized Audience for the Arts. Madison: Center for Arts Administration, Graduate School of Business, University of Wisconsin, 1976. 51p.

Johnson, Priscilla. Khrushchev and the Arts: The Politics of Soviet Culture, 1962-1964. Cambridge, Mass.: MIT Press, 1965. 300p.

Jowett, Garth. Film: The Democratic Art. Boston: Little, Brown, 1976. 518p.

Kepes, Gyorgy. Arts of the Environment. New York: G. Braziller, 1972. 244p.

Kranz, Stewart. The Fourth "R": Art for the Urban School. New York: Van Nostrand-Reinhold, 1970. 116p.

Kreitler, Hans, and Shulamith Kreitler. Psychology of the Arts. Durham, N.C.: Duke University Press, 1972. 514p.

McWhinney, William H., and James M. Woods. "Arts in the Neighborhood." Los Angeles: Graduate School of Management, University of California, 1973. 22p. (Management in the Arts Research Paper no. 19.)

Minihan, Janet. The Nationalization of Culture: The Development of State Subsidies to the Arts in Great Britain. New York: New York University Press, 1976. 288p.

Murphy, Judith, and Ronald Ross. The Arts and the Poor; New Challenges for Educators. Washington, D. C. : U. S. Office of Education, Bureau of Research, 1968. 42p.

Murphy, Judith, and Ronald Ross. The Place of the Arts in New Towns; A Report from Educational Facilities Laboratories. New York, 1973. 72p.

National Committee for Cultural Resources. "National Report on the Arts." New York, 1975. 36p.

National Council of YMCA's. Training Volunteer Leaders. Fairfax, Va. : NTL Learning Resources Corp. , 1974. 189p.

National Research Center of the Arts. Americans and the Arts: Highlights. New York: Associated Councils of the Arts, 1974. 36p.

National Research Center of the Arts. Americans and the Arts: A Survey of Public Opinion. New York: Associated Councils of the Arts, 1975. 162p.

National Research Center of the Arts. Museums, U. S. A. : A Survey Report. Washington, D. C. : National Endowment for the Arts, for sale by the Superintendent of Documents, 1975. 592p.

National Research Center of the Arts. A Study of the Nonprofit Arts and Cultural Industry of New York State. New York, 1972. 194p.

New York (City). Mayor's Committee on Cultural Policy. Report of the Mayor's Committee on Cultural Policy, October 15, 1974. New York, 1974. 87p.

New York (State). Commission on Cultural Resources. Arts

and the Schools: Patterns for Better Education; Report. Albany, 1972. 100p.

New York (State). Commission on Cultural Resources. Cultural Resource Development. New York: Praeger, 1976. 219p.

New York (State). State Council on the Arts. New York State Council on the Arts: Report. Annual.

Pasquill, Frank T., and Joan Horsman. Wooden Pennies: A Report on Cultural Funding Patterns in Canada. Toronto: York University, Programme in Arts Administration, 1973. 75p.

Peterson, Theodore Bernard, and Jay W. Jensen. The Mass Media and Modern Society. New York: Holt, Rinehart & Winston, 1965. 259p.

Schindler-Rainman, Eva, and Ronald Lippitt. Team Training for Community Change: Concepts, Goals, Strategies & Skills. Fairfax, Va.: NTL Learning Resources Corp., 1972. 75p.

A Seminar on the Role of the Arts in Meeting the Social and Educational Needs of the Disadvantaged; Final report. Hanna T. Rose, principal investigator. Brooklyn, N.Y.: Brooklyn Museum, 1967. 285p.

Shuker, Nancy, ed. Arts in Education Partners: Schools and Their Communities. New York: Associated Councils of the Arts, 1977. 125p.

The Sociology of the Arts. Edited by Mildred Weil and Duncan Hartley. Danville, Ill.: Interstate Printers & Publishers, 1975. 179p.

Steiner, George A. Business and Society. 2d ed. New York: Random House, 1975. 611p.

Steiner, George A. Issues in Business and Society. 2d ed. New York: Random House, 1977. 560p.

U.S. Department of Health, Education, and Welfare. Toward a Social Report. With an introductory commentary by Wilbur J. Cohen. Ann Arbor: University of Michigan Press, 1970. 101p.

Webber, Ross A. Culture and Management: Text and Readings in Comparative Management. Homewood, Ill. : Irwin, 1969. 598p.

Wells, Alan. Mass Media and Society. Palo Alto, Calif. : National Press Books, 1972. 407p.

XIV

THE THEATER

Arts Council of Great Britain. The Theatre Today in England
and Wales; The Report of the Arts Council Theatre Enquiry, 1970. London, 1970. 79p.

Arts in Society. Entire issue: The Theatre: Does It Exist?,
v. 8, no. 2, Fall-Winter 1971.

Billboard. Weekly. Lee Zhito, editor. Billboard Publications, Inc., 9000 Sunset Blvd., Los Angeles, Calif.
90069. Advertising; book, film, play, record, and
television reviews; Illustrations. Circulation: 35,339.

California Theater Index, 1971: College, University Facilities.
Los Angeles: Graduate School of Management, Univer-
sity of California, 1971. 46p. (Management in the Arts
Research Paper no. 3.)

Cavanaugh, Jim. Organization and Management of the Non-
professional Theatre, Including Backstage and Front-of-
House. New York: Richards Rosen Press, 1973. 176p.

Center Theatre Group. Box Office Guidelines. New York:
Foundation for the Extension and Development of the
American Professional Theatre, 1974. 44p.

Cheney, Sheldon. The Art Theatre: A Discussion of Its
Ideals, Its Organization, and Its Promise as a Correc-
tive for Present Evils in the Commercial Theatre (1917).
Reprint: St. Clair Shores, Mich.: Scholarly Press,
1970. 249p.

Cohen, Selma Jeanne. Dance as a Theatre Art: Source
Readings in Dance History from 1581 to the Present.
New York: Dodd, Mead, 1974. 224p.

Corrigan, Robert W. The Theatre in Search of a Fix. New York: Delacorte Press, 1973. 368p.

Dace, Wallace. Subsidies for the Theater; A Study of the Central European System of Financing Drama, Opera and Ballet, 1968-1970. Manhattan, Kansas: AG Press, 1972. 188p.

Dodrill, Charles W. "Theatre Management Selected Bibliography." Washington, D. C.: American Educational Theatre Association, 1966. 10p. Mimeo.

Eaton, Quaintance. Opera Production II: A Handbook. Minneapolis: University of Minnesota Press, 1974. 347p.

Educational Facilities Laboratories. The Arts in Found Places: A Report from EFL and the National Endowment for the Arts. New York, 1976. 138p.

Educational Facilities Laboratories. New Places for the Arts: A Report from EFL and the National Endowment for the Arts. New York, 1976. 75p.

Elsom, John. Theatre Outside London. New York: Macmillan, 1971. 232p.

Eustis, Morton Corcoran. B'way, Inc! The Theatre as a Business (1934). Reprint: New York: Benjamin Blom, 1971. 356p.

Farber, Donald C. Actor's Guide: What You Should Know About the Contracts You Sign. New York: DBS Publications, 1971. 134p.

Farber, Donald C. From Option to Opening. 3d ed., rev. New York: Drama Book Specialists, 1977. 144p.

Farber, Donald C. Producing on Broadway; A Comprehensive Guide. New York: DBS Publications, 1969. 399p.

Flanagan, Hallie. Arena; The History of the Federal Theater (1940). Reprint: New York: Benjamin Blom, 1965. 475p.

Ford Foundation. Finances of the Performing Arts. Volume I, A Survey of 166 Professional Nonprofit Resident Theaters, Operas, Symphonies, Ballets, and Modern

Dance Companies. Volume II, A Survey of the Characteristics and Attitudes of Audiences for Theater, Opera,
Symphony, and Ballet in 12 U. S. Cities. New York,
1974. 2 volumes.

Foundation for the Extension and Development of the American
Professional Theatre. Subscription Guidelines. New
York, 1975. Various pagings.

Gard, Robert E. ; Marston Balch, and Pauline B. Temkin.
Theater in America; Appraisal and Challenge for the
National Theatre Conference. Madison, Wis. : Dembar
Educational Research Services, 1968. 192p.

Goldman, William. The Season; A Candid Look at Broadway.
New York: Harcourt Brace & World, 1969. 432p.

Goodman, Richard Alan, and Mirta Samuelson. "An Exploration into the Administrative Support of the Creative
Process: The Theater Case. " Los Angeles: Graduate
School of Management, University of California, 1970.
13p. (Management in the Arts Research Paper no. 6.)

Goodman, Richard Alan, and Lawrence Peter Goodman.
"Theatre as a Temporary System. " Los Angeles:
Graduate School of Management, University of California,
1971. 15p. (Management in the Arts Research Paper
no. 14.)

Greenberger, Howard. The Off-Broadway Experience. Englewood Cliffs, N. J. : Prentice-Hall, 1971. 207p.

Gruver, Elbert A. The Stage Manager's Handbook. Rev. by
Frank Hamilton. New York: Drama Book Specialists,
1972. 220p.

Humanities and the Theatre; Final Report. A project of the
University Resident Theatre Association. Washington,
D. C. : American Theatre Association, 1973. 2 volumes.

Kaplan, Benjamin, and Ralph S. Brown, Jr. Cases on Copyright, Unfair Competition, and Other Topics Bearing on
the Protection of Literary, Musical, and Artistic Works.
2d ed. Mineola, N. Y. : Foundation Press, 1974. 997p.

Krawitz, Herman E. , with Howard K. Klein. Royal American
Symphonic Theater: A Radical Proposal for a Subsidized

Nonprofessional Theater. New York: Macmillan, 1975. 211p.

La Houd, John. Theater Reawakening: A Report on Ford Foundation Assistance to American Drama. New York: Ford Foundation, 1977. 44p.

Langley, Stephen. Theatre Management in America: Principle and Practice; Producing for the Commercial, Stock, Resident, College and Community Theatre. New York: Drama Book Specialists, 1974. 405p.

Little, Stuart W. Off-Broadway; The Prophetic Theater. New York: Coward, McCann & Geoghegan, 1972. 323p.

Little, Stuart W., and Arthur Cantor. The Playmakers. New York: W. W. Norton, 1970. 320p.

Lloyd, Kenneth Louis. "Adherence to Work Rules: A Case Study of the Professional Theatrical Actor in the Los Angeles Area. " Ph. D. dissertation, University of California Los Angeles, Graduate School of Management, 1972. 246p.

Minus, Johnny. The Managers', Entertainers', and Agents' Book; How to Plan, Plot, Scheme, Learn, Perform, Avoid Dangers, and Enjoy Your Career in the Entertainment Industry. Hollywood, Calif. : 7 Arts Press, 1971. 732p.

Moore, Thomas Gale. The Economics of the American Theater. Durham, N. C. : Duke University Press, 1968. 192p.

Morison, Bradley G. , and Kay Fliehr. In Search of an Audience; How an Audience Was Found for the Tyrone Guthrie Theatre. Commissioned by Associated Councils of the Arts. Preface by Sir Tyrone Guthrie. New York: Pitman, 1968. 229p.

National Endowment for the Arts. "Research Division Program Solicitation--Study of the Condition and Needs of the American Theatre. " Washington, D. C. , 1977. 35p.

Newman, Danny. Subscribe Now! Building Arts Audiences Through Dynamic Subscription Promotion. New York: Theatre Communications Group, 1977. 304p.

Osborne, Alfred E. Economics of the Performing Arts: A
    Bibliography (Mainly Theater). Los Angeles: Graduate
    School of Management, University of California, 1976.
    (Management in the Arts Research Paper no. 31.)

Poggi, Jack. Theater in America; The Impact of Economic
    Forces, 1870-1967. Ithaca, N.Y.: Cornell University
    Press, 1968. 328p.

Pride, Leo Bryan. International Theatre Directory; A World
    Directory of the Theatre and Performing Arts. New
    York: Simon & Schuster, 1973. 577p.

Prince, Harold S. Contradictions: Notes on Twenty-Six
    Years in the Theatre. New York: Dodd, Mead, 1974.
    242p.

Salem, Mahmoud. Organizational Survival in the Performing
    Arts: The Making of the Seattle Opera. New York:
    Praeger, 1976. 210p.

Simon, Louis M. A History of the Actors' Fund of America.
    New York: Theatre Arts Books, 1972. 274p.

Stern, Lawrence. Stage Management: A Guidebook of Prac-
    tical Techniques. Boston: Allyn and Bacon, 1974.
    323p.

Stoyle, Judith. Economic and Demographic Characteristics
    of Actors' Equity Association Membership. Philadelphia:
    Actors' Equity Association in cooperation with Bureau
    of Economic and Business Research, School of Business
    Administration, Temple University, of the Common-
    wealth System of Higher Education, 1970.

TCG Fiscal Survey. Annual. Prepared by James Copeland,
    program director. New York: Theatre Communications
    Group.

Theatre Profiles: An Informational Handbook of Nonprofit
    Professional Theatres in the United States. Bi-annual.
    Edited by Lindy Zesch and Marsue Cumming. New York:
    Theatre Communications Group, Inc.

The Theatrical Manager in England and America; Player of a
    Perilous Game; Philip Henslowe, Tate Wilkinson, Stephen
    Price, Edwin Booth, Charles Wyndham. Joseph W. Don-

ohue, Jr. , editor. Princeton, N. J. : Princeton University Press, 1971. 216p.

Variety. Weekly. Syd Silverman, editor. Variety, Inc. , 154 W. 46th St. , New York, N. Y. 10036. Advertising; film, music, play, radio, record, and television reviews.

Wechsberg, Joseph. The Opera. New York: Macmillan, 1972. 312p.

West Coast Theatrical Directory. Los Angeles: Tarcher/ Gousha Guides, 1973. 310p.

Zeigler, Joseph Wesley. Regional Theatre; The Revolutionary Stage. Minneapolis: University of Minnesota Press, 1973. 277p.

XV

THE VISUAL ARTS

American Architects Directory. 3d ed. New York: R. R.
    Bowker, 1970.

American Art Directory. New York: R. R. Bowker, 1974.
    457p.

The Anatomy of an Art Auction; A Vital Guide for Organiza-
    tion Fund Raisers. Commack, N. Y. : Arnold Harvey
    Associates, 1972. 77p.

Annual Art Sales Index. Weybridge, Surrey, England: Art
    Sales Index, Ltd.

Art at Auction: The Year at Sotheby's and Parke-Bernet.
    Annual, New York: Viking.

Art Price Annual. Munich: Kunst und Technik.

Art Prices Current. Annual. Folkestone, Kent, England:
    William Dawson & Sons.

Art Works: Law, Policy, Practice. Edited by Franklin
    Feldman and Stephen E. Weil. New York: Practising
    Law Institute, 1974. 1214p.

Artist and Computer. Edited by Ruth Leavitt. New York:
    Harmony Books, 1976. 121p.

Artist's Market '76. Edited by Kirk Polking and Liz Prince.
    Cincinnati: Writer's Digest, 1975. 624p.

Arts Council of Great Britain. Training Arts Administrators.
    Report of the Committee of Enquiry into Arts Adminis-
    tration Training. London, 1971. 76p.

Associated Councils of the Arts. Directory of National Arts
    Organizations. New York, 1972. 60p.

Associated Councils of the Arts. The Visual Artist and the
    Law. New York, 1971. 100p.

Bérard, Michèle. Encyclopedia of Modern Art Auction Prices.
    New York: Arco, 1971. 417p.

Berlye, Milton K. Selling Your Art Work: A Marketing
    Guide for Fine and Commercial Artists. South Bruns-
    wick, N. J. : A. S. Barnes, 1973. 272p.

Chamberlain, Betty. The Artist's Guide to His Market. 2d
    ed. New York: Watson-Guptill Publications, 1975.
    176p.

Christie's Review of the Season. Annual. London: St. Mar-
    tin's Press.

Contemporary Crafts Market Place. Irregular. Compiled by
    the American Crafts Council. Ann Arbor, Mich. : Bow-
    ker.

The Crafts Report. Monthly newsletter. Crafts Report Pub.
    Co. , Brooklyn, N. Y. 11230.

Dawson, William M. A Residency Handbook. Madison, Wis. :
    Association of College, University and Community Arts
    Administrators, 1975. 46p.

Eagle, Joanna. Buying Art on a Budget. New York: Award
    Books, 1970. 403p.

Educational Facilities Laboratories. The Arts in Found
    Places: A Report from EFL and the National Endow-
    ment for the Arts. New York, 1976. 138p.

Educational Facilities Laboratories. New Places for the Arts:
    A Report from EFL and the National Endowment for the
    Arts. New York, 1976. 75p.

Fine Arts Market Place. Biennial. Edited by Paul Cummings.
    New York: Bowker.

Goodman, Calvin J. , with Florence J. Goodman. Marketing
    Art: A Handbook for Artists and Art Dealers. Los
    Angeles: Gee Tee Bee, 1972. 318p.

Green, Dennis. % For Art: New Legislation Can Integrate

Art and Architecture. Edited by Brennan Rash. Denver: Western States Arts Foundation, 1976. 72p.

Hodes, Scott. What Every Artist and Collector Should Know About the Law. New York: Dutton, 1974. 268p.

International Art Market. Monthly. Howard L. Katzander, editor. Art in America, Inc., 150 E. 58th St. New York, N.Y. 10022. Advertising, illustrations, market prices, index. Circulation: 3000.

International Art Sales. Annual. New York: Crown Publishers.

International Auction Records. Annual. New York: Editions Publisol.

International Directory of Arts, 1969-1970. 10th edition. New York: Editions Publisol, 1970. 2 volumes, 1988p.

Kaplan, Benjamin, and Ralph S. Brown, Jr. Cases on Copyright, Unfair Competition, and Other Topics Bearing on the Protection of Literary, Musical, and Artistic Works. 2d ed. Mineola, N.Y.: The Foundation Press, 1974. 997p.

Keen, Geraldine. Money and Art; A Study Based on the Times-Sotheby Index. New York: G. P. Putnam, 1971. 286p.

Levy, Julien. Memoir of an Art Gallery. New York: Putnam, 1977. 320p.

Magnan, George A. Using Technical Art; An Industry Guide. New York: Wiley-Interscience, 1970. 236p.

Mason, Lauris. Print Reference Sources: Select Bibliography, 18th-20th Centuries. Millwood, N.Y.: Kraus Thomson, 1974.

Meyer, Karl-Ernst. The Plundered Past; The Story of the Illegal International Traffic in Works of Art. New York: Atheneum, 1973. 353p.

Middlemas, Robert Keith. The Double Market: Art Theft and Art Thieves. Farnborough, England: Saxon House, 1975. 237p.

Osborne, Harold, editor. The Oxford Companion to Art. Oxford: Clarendon Press, 1970. 1277p.

Photography Market Place. 2d ed. Edited by Fred W. McDarrah. Ann Arbor, Mich.: Bowker, 1977. 475p.

Schiff, Bennett. Artists in Schools. Washington, D. C.: National Endowment for the Arts, 1973. 190p.

Scott, Michael. The Crafts Business Encyclopedia: Marketing, Management, and Money. New York: Harcourt Brace Jovanovich, 1977. 286p.

Strauss, Victor. Graphic Arts Management. Designed and illustrated by Edith Strauss. Philadelphia: Presentation Press, 1973. 340p.

Tamarind Lithography Workshop. Sex Differentials in Art Exhibition Reviews: A Statistical Study. Los Angeles, 1972. 132p.

Towner, Wesley. The Elegant Auctioneers. Completed by Stephen Varble. New York: Hill & Wang, 1970. 632p.

The Visual Artist and the Law. Rev. ed. New York: Praeger, 1974. 87p.

Voegeli, Thomas J. Handbook for Tour Management. Madison: Center for Arts Administration, Graduate School of Business, University of Wisconsin, 1975. 55p.

Wayne, June. New Careers in the Arts. Los Angeles: Tamarind Lithography Workshop, 1966. 6p.

Wayne, June. The Selling of Art. Los Angeles: Tamarind Lithography Workshop, 1966. 12p.

White, Jan V. Editing by Design; Word and Picture Communication for Editors and Designers. New York: R. R. Bowker, 1973. 230p.

Who's Who in American Art. New York: R. R. Bowker, 1973. 927p.

World Collector's Annuary. Voorburg, The Netherlands: World Collectors Publishers.

XVI

VOLUNTEERISM

American Institute of Certified Public Accountants. Committee
on Voluntary Health and Welfare Organizations. Audits
of Voluntary Health and Welfare Organizations. New
York, 1974. 51p.

Comish, Newel W. Effective Leadership of Voluntary Organizations. Winter Park, Fla. : Anna Publishing, 1976.
205p.

Conrad, William, and Glenn, William. The Effective Voluntary Board of Directors. Chicago: Swallow, 1976.
185p.

Cull, John G. , and Richard E. Hardy. Volunteerism: An
Emerging Profession. Springfield, Ill. : Charles C.
Thomas, 1973. 100p.

Feinstein, Barbara, and Catherine Cavanaugh. The New Volunteerism: A Community Connection. Cambridge,
Mass. : Schenkman Pub. Co. , 1976. 178p.

Final Report of the Institute for Community Service. Minneapolis: Lutheran Social Services of Minnesota, 1973.
64p.

"Handbook for Agency Coordinators for Volunteer Programs. "
New York: Voluntary Action Center for New York City,
Mayor's Office for Volunteers, 1972. 20p.

Hardy, Richard E. , and John G. Cull. Applied Volunteerism
in Community Development. Springfield, Ill. : Charles
C. Thomas, 1973. 227p.

Hartogs, Nelly, and Joseph Weber. Boards of Directors: A

Study of Current Practices in Board Management and Board Operations in Voluntary Hospitals, Health and Welfare Organizations. Sponsored by the Greater New York Fund, Inc. Dobbs Ferry, N. Y. : Oceana, 1974. 266p.

Institute for Community Service Manual: A Process for Developing Agency-Based Volunteer Social Work Staff. Minneapolis: Lutheran Social Services of Minnesota, 1973. 122p.

Kerri, James Nwannukwu. "Voluntary Associations in Change and Conflict--A Bibliography." Monticello, Ill. : Council of Planning Librarians, 1974. (Council of Planning Librarians Exchange Bibliography no. 551.)

Journal of Voluntary Action Research. Quarterly. Association of Voluntary Action Scholars, Box G-55, Boston College, Chestnut Hill, Mass. 02167.

Lehmann, Clara, and Dolores Glenn. The Intriguing World of Modern Management. New York: Vantage Press, 1977. 328p.

Manser, Gordon, and Rosemary Higgins Cass. Voluntarism at the Crossroads. New York: Family Service Association of America, 1976. 262p.

Miller, Ruby Sills. Helping the Volunteer Get Started: The Role of the Volunteer Center. Washington, D. C. : National Center for Voluntary Action, 1972. 90p.

National Center for Voluntary Action. "Clearinghouse Green Sheets." Annual. (Annotated listing of resource groups and publications in specific volunteer areas as well as related areas that complement the volunteer information). Washington, D. C.

Naylor, Harriet. Volunteers Today. Dryden, N. Y. : Dryden Associates, 1973. 195p.

O'Connell, Brian. Effective Leadership in Voluntary Organizations: How to Make the Greatest Use of Citizen Service and Influence. New York: Association Press, 1976. 202p.

Okin, Tessie, and Carolyn Wiener. Planning, Implementing,

Evaluating a Workshop for Directors of Volunteers. Washington, D. C. :　National Center for Voluntary Action, 1973.　68p.

Pell, Arthur R.　Recruiting, Training and Motivating Volunteer Workers.　New York:　Pilot Books, 1972.　63p.

Routh, Thomas A.　The Volunteer and Community Agencies. Springfield, Ill. :　Charles C. Thomas, 1972.　92p.

Schindler-Rainman, Eva, and Ronald Lippitt.　The Volunteer Community:　Creative Use of Human Resources.　2d ed. Fairfax, Va. :　Learning Resources Corp. , 1975.　176p.

Smith, Constance, and Anne Freedman.　Voluntary Associations:　Perspectives on the Literature.　Cambridge, Mass. :　Harvard University Press, 1972.　250p.

Stenzel, Anne K. , and Helen M. Feeney.　Volunteer Training and Development:　A Manual for Community Groups. New York:　Seabury Press, 1968.　223p.

Training Volunteer Leaders:　A Handbook to Train Volunteers and Other Leaders of Program Groups.　New York: Research and Development Division, National Council of Young Men's Christian Associations, 1974.　189p.

Trecker, Harleigh B.　Citizen Boards at Work:　New Challenges to Effective Action.　New York:　Association Press, 1970.　288p.

Voluntary Action Leadership.　Quarterly.　National Center for Voluntary Action, 1785 Massachusetts Ave. , NW, Washington, D. C.　20036.

Voluntary Action Research.　Annual.　Lexington, Mass. : Lexington Books, D. C. Heath.

Voluntary Associations.　Edited by J. Roland Pennack and John W. Chapman.　New York:　Lieber-Atherton, 1969. 291p.

Volunteer Administration.　Quarterly.　Association of Voluntary Action Scholars, Box G-55, Boston College, Chestnut Hill, Mass.　02167.

Your Volunteer Program.　Ankeny, Iowa:　Des Moines Area Community College, Project Motivate, 1970.　300p.

Wattel, Harold L. , ed. Voluntarism and the Business Community. Hempstead, N. Y. : Hofstra University, 1971. 589p. (Hofstra University Yearbook of Business, series 8, v. 1.)

Wilson, Marlene. The Effective Management of Volunteer Programs. Boulder, Colo. : Volunteer Management Associates, 1976. 197p.

XVII

INDEXES TO
JOURNALS, NEWSLETTERS, AND NEWSPAPERS

There is unlimited information on all aspects of the
arts and administration to be found in periodical literature: journals, magazines, newspapers, newsletters, and all the various other kinds of serial
publications. A variety of indexes provide access
to this material. The following titles are suggested
as being the most helpful. Suggested subject headings
are listed under each index title given.

Art Index. Quarterly with annual cumulations. H. W. Wilson
    Co., 950 University Ave., Bronx, N.Y. 10452.
    Art / Management / Museum Personnel / Museums
    and Art Galleries--Administration

Business Periodicals Index. Monthly, except August, with
    annual cumulations. H. W. Wilson Co., 950 University
    Ave., Bronx, N.Y. 10452.
    The Arts--Management / Foundations, Charitable and
    Educational / Museums / Performing Arts

Dissertation Abstracts International. (Formerly Dissertation
    Abstracts.) Monthly with annual index volume. Univer-
    sity Microfilms, 300 N. Zeeb Road, Ann Arbor, Mich.
    48106. This index to doctoral dissertations is issued in
    two parts, of which Section A, Humanities and Social
    Sciences, is pertinent to the subject of the bibliography
    under such subject headings as:
    Art Patronage / Management / Music--Economic
    Aspects / Performing Arts--U. S. --Finance / State En-
    couragement of Science, Literature and Art / Theaters--
    Organization

    University Microfilms also publishes American Doctoral
    Dissertations.

Guide to the Performing Arts. Covers 1957 through 1968.
(Ceased publication; formerly published as a supplement
to Guide to the Musicial Arts; superseded Guide to
Dance Periodicals) Metuchen, N. J. : Scarecrow Press.
  Copyright / Dance as Business / Labor and Laboring
Classes / Music--Economic Aspects / Music Industry /
Orchestras

Index to Legal Periodicals. Monthly, October-August; annual
and three-year cumulations. An author and subject in-
dex to legal periodicals and journals. H. W. Wilson
Co. , 950 University Ave. , Bronx, N. Y. 10452.
  Censorship / Copyright / Entertainment / Foundations /
Law in Arts and Literature / Taxation

Music Index. Monthly with annual cumulation. A subject-
author guide to over 270 current periodicals from the
U. S. , England, Canada, Australia, and 19 non-English
language countries. Entries are in the language of the
country of origin. Information Coordinators, Inc. ,
1435 Randolph St. , Detroit, Mich. 48226.
  Ballet / Business and Performing Arts / Dance /
Opera / Symphony Orchestras--Financing; --Management

New York Times Index. 24 semi-monthly issues with an an-
nual cumulative index. New York Times Company.
Subject indexing is complete, detailed, and explicit.
Look under all entries related to subject-at-hand.

Public Affairs Information Service. Bulletin. Weekly, Sep-
tember-July; fortnightly, August; cumulated five times
a year and annually. An index to publications (books,
journals, pamphlets, and government documents) relating
to economic and social affairs. Public Affairs Information Service, Inc. , 11 West 40th St. , New York, N. Y.
10018.
  Actors / Art / Museums / Music / Orchestras /
Performing Arts / Theater

U. S. Government Printing Office. Monthly Catalog [of Publi-
cations]. A semi-annual index is published following the
June issue each year and the December issue includes
an annual index.
  Art / Drama / Museums / Music / National Foundation on the Arts and Humanities / Symphony Orchestras

See Associations, Councils, and Other Organizations (page

113) below for publications of the various associations, councils and other organizations.

In addition, Ulrich's International Periodicals Directory, A Classified Guide to Current Periodicals Domestic and Foreign, 17th ed. , Bowker, 1977-78, "includes entries for over 60,000 in print periodicals published throughout the world. " Irregular Serials & Annuals: An International Directory, 4th ed. , Bowker, 1976-77, also "provides bibliographic and buying information for approximately 30,000 serials currently published throughout the world. " The titles are arranged according to subject, i.e. , Art Galleries and Museums, Business, Management, Music, Theatre, etc.

XVIII

JOURNALS, NEWSLETTERS, AND NEWSPAPERS

No individual journal articles are cited as such in
this bibliography. Literally hundreds of pertinent
entries can be found using the indexes listed in Part
XVII and in the selected titles listed below.

AADC Newsletter. Irregular. Association of American
Dance Companies, 162 W. 56th St. , New York, N. Y.
10019.

ACA Reports. 1968. Bi-monthly. Ellen S. Daniels, editor.
Associated Councils of the Arts, 570 Seventh Ave. ,
New York, N. Y. 10018. Book reviews, charts, illus-
trations, statistics. Circulation controlled.

ACA Word from Washington. 1972. Monthly. Jack Golod-
ner, editor. Associated Councils of the Arts, 570
Seventh Ave. , New York, N. Y. 10018.

American Artist Business Letter. 1974. Monthly except
July and August. David Preiss, editor. American Ar-
tist Magazine, 1515 Broadway, New York, N. Y. 10036.
Circulation: 5000.

American Music Center. Newsletter. 1959. Quarterly.
Miriam S. Michel, editor. American Music Center,
Suite 626-7, 250 W. 57th St. , New York, N. Y. 10019.
Advertising. Circulation: 1000.

Art Investment Report. Fortnightly. Richard H. Rush, edi-
torial director. Wall Street Reports Pub. Co. , 120
Wall St. , New York, N. Y. 10005.

Art News. 1902. Monthly, September-May; quarterly, June-
August. Milton Esterow, editor. Artnews, 750 Third

Ave., New York, N. Y. 10017. Advertising, book reviews, illustrations. Circulation: 50,000. Indexed in
Art Index.

Art Workers News. 1971 (Formerly Art Workers Newsletter.)
Monthly, 10 issues per year. Foundation for the Community of Artists, 32 Union Square East, New York,
N. Y. 10003. Advertising, book reviews, bibliographies,
illustrations. Circulation: 10,000. Tabloid format.

Arts Advocate. 1974-1976 (ceased publication). Quarterly,
membership. Advocates for the Arts, John Hightower,
chairman, New York.

Arts and the Law. 10 times per year. Volunteer Lawyers
for the Arts, Suite 1110, 36 W. 44th St., New York,
N. Y. 10036.

Arts in Society. 1958-1976 (ceased publication with v. 13,
no. 2, 1976). Edward L. Kamarck, editor. University
of Wisconsin Extension. Advertising, book reviews, illustrations, index. Circulation was 5000.

Arts Management. 1962. 5 times per year. Alvin H. Reiss,
editor. Radius Group, Inc., 408 W. 57th St., New
York, N. Y. 10019. Book reviews, statistics, index.
Circulation: 12,000.

Arts Reporting Service. 1970. Fortnightly. Charles C.
Mark, editor. 9214 Three Oaks Dr., Silver Spring,
Md. 20901. Book reviews. Circulation: 1500.

Association of College, University and Community Arts Ad-
ministrators. Bulletin. 1958. Monthly. Miriam
Boegel, editor. Association of College, University and
Community Arts Administrators, Box 2137. Madison,
Wis. 53701. Book reviews. Circulation: 450.

Association Management. 1949. Monthly. Elaine Jorpeland,
editor. American Society of Association Executives,
1101 16th St., NW, Washington, D. C. 20036. Advertisements, book reviews, illustrations, index. Circulation: 8000. (Indexed in the Public Affairs Information
Service Bulletin.)

Auction. 1967. Monthly. Linda Rosencrantz, editor. 980
Madison Ave., New York, N. Y. 10021. Book reviews,
advertising, illustrations.

Aviso. 1968. Monthly. Carol Bannerman, editor. American Association of Museums, 1055 Thomas Jefferson
St., NW, Washington, D. C. 20007.

BCA News. 1968. Quarterly. Michael d'Amelio, editor.
Business Committee for the Arts, 1700 Broadway, New
York, N. Y. 10019. Illustrations, statistics. Circula-
tion: 13, 000.

Billboard. 1894. Weekly. Lee Zhito, editor. Billboard
Publications, Inc., 9000 Sunset Blvd., Los Angeles,
Calif. 90069. Advertising; drama, television, film,
record and book reviews; illustrations. Circulation:
35,339. (Indexed in Music Index.)

Business and Society; A Journal of Interdisciplinary Exploration. 1960. Twice annually. Bismarck Williams, editor. Walter E. Heller College of Business Administration, Roosevelt University, 430 South Michigan Ave.,
Chicago, Ill. 60605. Trade literature. Circulation:
3500. (Indexed in Public Affairs Information Service
Bulletin.)

Business Screen. 1938. Bi-monthly. Bob Seymour, editor.
Harcourt Brace Jovanovich, Inc., 757 Third Ave. New
York, N. Y. 10017. Advertisements; book and film re-
views; illustrations. Circulation: 13, 000 (controlled).

Business Week. 1929. Weekly. Lewis H. Young, editor.
McGraw-Hill, Inc., 1221 Ave. of the Americas, New
York, N. Y. 10020. Advertising, book reviews, illus-
trations, statistics, index. Circulation: 750, 000. (In-
dexed in Business Periodicals Index and Public Affairs
Information Service Bulletin.)

Cultural Affairs. 1967-1971 (ceased publication). Quarterly.
Peter Spackman, editor. Associated Councils of the
Arts, New York. Illustrations. Circulation was con-
trolled.

Cultural Post. 1975. Bi-monthly. George Clack, editor.
National Endowment for the Arts, Washington, D. C.
20506. Bibliographies, illustrations. Tabloid format.

Daedalus. 1958. Quarterly. Stephen R. Graubard, editor.
American Academy of Arts and Sciences, 165 Allendale
St. Jamaica Plains Station, Boston, Mass. 02130.

Charts, illustrations, index. Circulation: 58,000. (Indexed in Public Affairs Information Service Bulletin.)
See especially v. 98, no. 1, Winter 1969. "Perspectives of Business."

Dance. 1926. Monthly. William Como, editor. Danad Pub. Co., 10 Columbus Circle, New York, N.Y. 10019. Advertising; book, film, and drama reviews; illustrations. Circulation: 40,000.

Dance/America. 1972. Quarterly. Doris Hering, editor. National Association for Regional Ballet, 1860 Broadway, New York, N.Y. 10023. Book and film reviews, illustrations. Circulation: 5000.

Dance Research Journal. 1967. Semi-annual. Ruth Kramoris, editor. Committee on Research in Dance, Dance Department, Education 675D, New York University, 35 W. 4th St., New York, N.Y. 10003. Book and film reviews, abstracts, bibliographies, charts, illustrations.

Drama Review; New Plays and Translations, Criticism, Theory, Reviews, Interviews. 1955. Quarterly. Michael Kirby, editor. New York University, School of the Arts, Room 300, 51 W. 4th St., New York, N.Y. 10012. Advertising, bibliographies, book and drama reviews, charts, illustrations, index. Circulation: 10,000.

Educational Theatre Journal. 1949. Quarterly. Anthony Graham-White, editor. American Theatre Association, 1317 F St., NW, Washington, D.C. 20004. Advertising, book and drama reviews, charts, illustrations, statistics, index. Circulation to membership: 6000.

Fortune. 1930. Monthly. Robert Lubar, editor. Time, Inc., 591 N. Fairbanks Court, Chicago, Ill. 60611. Advertising, illustrations, book essays. Circulation: 515,000. (Indexed in Business Periodicals Index, and Public Affairs Information Service Bulletin.)

Foundation Center Information Quarterly. October 1972-July 1974 (ceased publication). Foundation Center, 888 7th Ave., New York, N.Y. 10019.

Foundation News. 1960. Bi-monthly. Patrick W. Kennedy, editor. Council on Foundations, Inc., 888 Seventh Ave. (P.O. Box 783, Old Chelsea Station), New York, N.Y. 10019. Book reviews, index. Circulation: 10,000.

Fund Raising Management. 1969. Bi-monthly. John Mc-
Ilquham, editor. Hoke Communications, 224 Seventh
St., Garden City, N. Y. 11530. Advertising, book re-
views, illustrations. Circulation: 10, 000.

Grantsmanship Center News. 8 issues per year. Thomas T.
Whitney, editor. Grantsmanship Center, Los Angeles,
Calif. 90015. Book reviews, index. Circulation:
10, 500.

International Musician. 1901. Monthly. J. Martin Emerson,
editor. American Federation of Musicians of the United
States and Canada, 1500 Broadway, New York, N. Y.
10036. Advertising, illustrations. Circulation: 305, 000.
Tabloid format. (Indexed in Music Index.)

Journal of Voluntary Action Research. 1972. Quarterly.
David Horton Smith, editor. Association of Voluntary
Action Scholars, Box G-55, Boston College, Chestnut
Hill, Mass. 02167. Index. Circulation: 600.

Kennedy Center News. Bi-monthly. Kennedy Center for the
Performing Arts, Washington, D. C. 20566.

Museum News. 1924. Bi-monthly. Ellen C. Hicks, editor.
American Association of Museums, 1055 Thomas Jefferson St., NW, Washington, D. C. 20007. Advertising,
book reviews, illustrations, index. Circulation: 6000.

Music Journal; Educational Music Magazine. 1943. Monthly,
September-June. Hannah Hanani, editor. Music Jour-
nal, Inc., 20 Hampton Rd., Southampton, N. Y. 11968.
Advertising, book reviews. Circulation: 20, 000-22, 000.
(Indexed in Music Index.)

National Society of Fund Raisers Newsletter. 11 issues per
year. 17 E. 48th St., New York, N. Y. 10017.

Opera Journal. 1968. Quarterly. Leland S. Fox, editor.
National Opera Association, University of Mississippi,
Division of Continuing Education and Extension, University, Miss. 38677. Book and music reviews, illustrations. Circulation: 1000.

Opera News. 1936. Monthly, May-November; weekly, De-
cember-April. Robert Jacobson, editor. Metropolitan
Opera Guild, 1865 Broadway, New York, N. Y. 10023.

Advertising, book reviews, bibliographies, illustrations, music and record reviews. Circulation: 85,000. (Indexed in Music Index.)

Performing Arts Journal. 1976. 3 times per year. Bonnie Marranca and Guatam Dasgupta, editors. Box 858, Peter Stuyvesant Station, New York, N.Y. 10009. Advertisements, book reviews, illustrations. Circulation: 2500.

Performing Arts Review; Journal of Management and Law of the Arts. 1969. Quarterly. Joseph Taubman, editor. Law-Arts Publishers, Inc., 453 Greenwich St., New York, N.Y. 10013. Advertisements, book reviews, charts, illustrations, statistics, index. Circulation: 2000. (Indexed in Index to Legal Periodicals.)

Symphony News. 1950. Bi-monthly. Benjamin S. Dunham, editor. American Symphony Orchestra League, Symphony Hill, Box 669, Vienna, Va. 22180. Advertising, book reviews, illustrations. Circulation: 10,000. (Indexed in Music Index.)

Theatre Design and Technology; News on the Construction of Theatres, New Technical Developments, Stage Design, Lighting, Sound, Administration. 1965. Quarterly. United States Institute for Theatre Technology, 1501 Broadway, New York, N.Y. 10036. Bibliographies, book and drama reviews, charts, illustrations, patents. Circulation to membership: 1620.

Variety. 1905. Weekly. Syd Silverman, editor. Variety, Inc., 154 W. 46th St., New York, N.Y. 10036. Advertisements; film, drama, music, radio, record and television reviews. (Indexed in Music Index.)

Voluntary Action Leadership. 1970. (Incorporating Voluntary Action News since 1976). Bi-monthly. Ted Orme, editor. National Center for Voluntary Action, 1785 Massachusetts Ave. NW, Washington, D.C. 20036. Book reviews. Circulation: 22,000. Tabloid format.

Volunteer Administration. Quarterly. Association of Voluntary Action Scholars, Box G-55, Boston College, Chestnut Hill, Mass. 02167.

Washington International Arts Letter. 1962. 10 times per

year. Daniel Millsaps, editor. Allied Business Con-
sultants, Inc. , Box 9005, Washington, D. C. 20003.
Book reviews, charts, illustrations. Circulation: 16,359.

XIX

REFERENCE SOURCES

ACA Arts Yellow Pages. Prepared by Margot Honig with the
    assistance of Raymond Baron. New York: Associated
    Councils of the Arts, 1977. 127p.

American Architects Directory. Annual. New York: Ameri-
    can Institute of Architects.

American Art Directory. Triennial. Jacques Cattell Press,
    editor. New York: Bowker.
        Covers various organizations (museums, art schools,
    college and university art departments) as well as inclu-
    ding sections on art magazines and newspapers with art
    coverage, scholarships and fellowships in the field, tra-
    velling exhibits, etc.

Associated Councils of the Arts. "Arts Centers in the United
    States. " New York, 1968. 11p. , mimeo.

Associated Councils of the Arts. "Directory of Community
    Arts Councils. " New York, 1972. 51p. , mimeo.
        Names, addresses, programming information on over
    200 community arts councils across the country. It
    tells what they do, how they are financed, who staffs
    them, what their problems are.

Associated Councils of the Arts. Directory of National Arts
    Organizations. New York, 1972. 60p.
        A second edition of ACA's guide to the national non-
    profit service organizations that serve major art forms:
    information on membership, purposes, activities, con-
    ferences, publications, and budgets. A directory de-
    signed to facilitate the exchange of information on ser-
    vices and programs available to the arts on a national
    level.

Associated Councils of the Arts. Directory of State Arts
    Councils. New York. Annual.

Associated Councils of the Arts. State Arts Councils. New
    York, Councils of the Arts, 1972. 86p.
    The first comprehensive report on the acts of 50 state
    councils, the District of Columbia, and the Virgin Islands.
    The data covers sources and amounts of funds received,
    the programs on which the funds were spent, as well as
    membership staffing of the councils and major issues of
    concern. Current list of chairmen and executive directors
    of all councils included.

Audiovisual Marketplace; A Multimedia Guide. Annual. New
    York: Bowker.

Bérard, Michèle. Encyclopedia of Modern Art Auction Prices.
    New York: Arco, 1971. 417p.

Broadcasting Cable Sourcebook. Annual. Washington, D. C. :
    Broadcasting Publications.

Broadcasting Yearbook. Annual. Washington, D. C. : Broad-
    casting Publications.

California. Arts Commission. The California Dance Direc-
    tory. Presented by the California Arts Commission and
    the Association of American Dance Companies. Sacra-
    mento, 1972. 78p.

California Theater Index 1971: College, University Facilities.
    Los Angeles: Graduate School of Management, Univer-
    sity of California, 1971. 46p. (Management in the
    Arts Research Papers no. 3.)

Contemporary Crafts Market Place. Irregular. Compiled by
    the American Crafts Council. Ann Arbor, Mich.: Bow-
    ker.

Costner, Tom. Motion Picture Market Place, 1976-1977.
    Boston: Little, Brown, 1976. 513p.

Cultural Directory: Guide to Federal Funds and Services for
    Cultural Activities. Research conducted by Linda Coe.
    New York: Associated Councils of the Arts, 1975. 356p.
    (Originally published in 1971 under title, Washington and
    the Arts.)

Directory of National Unions and Employee Associations. Bi-
    ennial. Washington: U. S. Bureau of Labor Statistics.

Encyclopedia of Associations. Irregular. 11th ed. , Margaret
    Fisk, editor. Detroit: Gale Research Company, 1977.
    3 volumes.

Fine Arts Market Place. Biennial. Edited by Paul Cummings.
    New York: Bowker.

The Focal Encyclopedia of Film and Television Techniques.
    Edited by Raymonde Spottiswoode. New York: Hastings
    House, 1969. 1100p.

Foundation Center. The Foundation Center National Data Book,
    1974-76. New York, 1977. 2 volumes.

Foundation Center. Foundation Center Source Book Profiles.
    New York, 1977- (distributed by Columbia University
    Press). Looseleaf.

Foundation Center. Foundation Directory. Marianna O.
    Lewis, editor. 6th ed. New York, 1977 (distributed
    by Columbia University Press), 661p.

Foundation Center. Foundation Grants to Individuals. New
    York, 1977. 227p.

Goodman, Calvin J. , with Florence J. Goodman. Marketing
    Art: A Handbook for Artists and Art Dealers. Los
    Angeles: Gee Tee Bee, 1972. 318p.

Handbook of Museums: Germany, Austria, Switzerland.
    (Handbuch der Museen: Deutschland BRD, DDR, Oster-
    reich, Schweiz.) Munich: Verlag Dokumentation, 1971.
    2 volumes.

Hudson, Kenneth, and Ann Nicholls. Directory of World
    Museums. New York: Columbia University Press,
    1975. 864p.

International Auction Records. Annual. New York: Editions
    Publisol.

International Directory of Arts. Biennial. New York: Edi-
    tions Publisol.

International Index to Film Periodicals. Irregular. New York: Bowker.

International Motion Picture Almanac. Annual. New York: Quigley Publications.

International Television Almanac. Annual. New York: Quigley Publications.

Lewis, Ralph H. Manual for Museums. Washington, D. C. : National Park Service, U. S. Department of the Interior, 1976. 412p.

Libraries, Museums and Art Galleries Yearbook. Irregular. New York: Bowker.

McCoy, Garnett. Archives in American Art; A Directory of Resources. New York: R. R. Bowker, 1972. 163p.

Mason, Lauris. Print Reference Sources: Select Bibliography, 18th-20th Centuries. Millwood, N. Y. : Kraus Thomson, 1974.

Museums of the World. Museen der Welt. Munich: Verlag Dokumentation, 1973. 762p.

National Center for Voluntary Action. "Clearinghouse Green Sheets. " Annual. (Annotated listing of resource groups and publications in specific volunteer areas as well as related areas that complement the volunteer information). Washington, D. C.

National Directory for the Performing Arts and Civic Centers. Edited by Beatrice Handel, Janet Spencer and Nolanda Turner. Dallas: Handel, 1975. 972p.

National Directory for the Performing Arts/Educational. Edited by Beatrice Handel, Nolanda Turner and Janet Spencer. Dallas: Handel, 1975. 821p.

The Official Museum Directory: United States, Canada. Biennial. Washington, D. C. : American Association of Museums.
    Geographically arranged lists of art, history, and science museums, giving names of directors and department heads, addresses, telephone numbers, hours, publications, major collections and special activities.

Osborne, Harold, editor. The Oxford Companion to Art. Oxford: Clarendon Press, 1970. 1277p.

Photography Market Place. 2d ed. Edited by Fred W. McDarrah. Ann Arbor, Mich.: Bowker, 1977. 475p.

Pride, Leo Bryan. International Theatre Directory; A World Directory of the Theatre and Performing Arts. New York: Simon & Schuster, 1973. 577p.

Prieve, E. Arthur, and Ira W. Allen. Administration in the Arts: An Annotated Bibliography of Selected References. Madison: Center for Arts Administration, Graduate School of Business, University of Wisconsin, 1973. 111p.

Private Foundations and Business Corporations Active in Arts/ Humanities/Education. By Daniel Millsaps and the editors of the Washington International Arts Letter. Washington, D.C.: Washington International Arts Letter, v. 1, 1970, 138p; v. 2, 1974, 264p.

Reiss, Alvin H. The Arts Management Handbook; A Guide for Those Interested in or Involved with the Administration of Cultural Institutions. Rev. ed. With a preface by Nancy Hanks. New York: Law-Arts Publishers, 1974. 802p.

Sadoul, Georges. Dictionary of Film Makers. Translated, edited and up-dated by Peter Morris. Berkeley: University of California Press, 1972. 288p.

Sadoul, Georges. Dictionary of Films. Translated, edited and up-dated by Peter Morris. Berkeley: University of California Press, 1972. 432p.

Schoolcraft, Ralph Newman. Performing Arts/Books in Print: An Annotated Bibliography. New York: Drama Book Specialists, 1973. 761p.

Scott, Michael. The Crafts Business Encyclopedia: Marketing, Management, and Money. New York: Harcourt Brace Jovanovich, 1977. 286p.

Theatre Profiles: An Informational Handbook of Nonprofit Professional Theatres in the United States. Bi-annual. Edited by Lindy Zesch and Marsue Cumming. New York: Theatre Communications Group, Inc.

Touring Directory of the Performing Arts in Canada. Ottawa: Information Canada, 1975.

Training Volunteer Leaders: A Handbook to Train Volunteers and Other Leaders of Program Groups. New York: Research and Development Division, National Council of Young Men's Christian Associations, 1974. 189p.

Truitt, Evelyn Mack. Who Was Who on the Screen. New York: Bowker, 1974. 363p.

Voluntary Action Research. Annual. Lexington, Mass.: Lexington Books, D. C. Heath.

Wasserman, Paul. Awards, Honors, and Prizes. Associate editor, Janice McLean. 3rd ed. Detroit: Gale Research Co., 1975. 2v.

Wasserman, Paul, and Esther Herman, editors. Museum Media; A Biennial Directory and Index of Publications and Audiovisuals Available from United States and Canadian Institutions. Detroit: Gale Research Company.

West Coast Theatrical Directory. Los Angeles: Tarcher/ Gousha Guides, 1973. 310p.

Who's Who in American Art. New York: R. R. Bowker, 1973. 927p.

XX

BIBLIOGRAPHIES

Blum, Eleanor. Basic Books in the Mass Media; An Annotated, Selected Booklist Covering General Communications, Book Publishing, Broadcasting, Film, Magazines, Newspapers, Advertising, Indexes, and Scholarly and Professional Periodicals. Urbana: University of Illinois, 1972. 252p.

Coe, Linda, and Stephen Benedict, comps. Arts Management: An Annotated Bibliography. Washington, D. C. : National Endowment for the Arts, Cultural Resources Development Project, 1978. unpaged.

Dodrill, Charles W. "Theatre Management Selected Bibliography. " Washington, D. C. : American Educational Theatre Association, 1966. 10p. , mimeo.

Georgi, Charlotte. Foundations, Grants & Fund-Raising: A Selected Bibliography. Los Angeles: Graduate School of Management, University of California, 1976. 67p.

Kaderlan, Norman. "Bibliography on the Administration of the Arts, 1958-1969. " Madison: University of Wisconsin Arts Council, 1969. 24p. , mimeo.

Kerri, James Nwannukwu. "Voluntary Associations in Change and Conflict--A Bibliography. " Monticello, Ill. : Council of Planning Librarians, 1974. 13p. (Council of Planning Librarians Exchange Bibliography no. 551.)

Levene, Victoria E. , and William J. Buckley. A Bibliography on Arts Administration. Binghamton, N. Y. : State University of New York at Binghamton, School of Management, School of Arts and Sciences, 1977. 30p.

National Endowment for the Arts. <u>Arts Library Acquisitions</u> <u>List.</u> Monthly. Washington, D. C.

Prieve, E. Arthur, and Ira W. Allen. <u>Administration in the</u> <u>Arts:</u> An Annotated Bibliography of Selected References. Madison: University of Wisconsin, Graduate School of Business, Center for Arts Administration, 1973. 111p.

Quint, Barbara and Lois Newman. "Performing Arts Centers and Economic Aspects of the Performing Arts: A Selective Bibliography. " Santa Monica, Calif. : Rand Corp. , 1969. 13p.

Schoolcraft, Ralph Newman. <u>Performing Arts/Books in Print:</u> <u>An Annotated Bibliography.</u> New York: Drama Book Specialists, 1973. 761p.

Whalon, Marion K. <u>Performing Arts Research: A Guide to</u> <u>Information Sources.</u> Detroit: Gale Research, 1976. 280p.

See Associations, Councils, and Other Organizations, (next page) for addresses to write to request lists of publications.

It is also noted that many of the books listed throughout the present work include excellent bibliographies: for example, Baumol and Bowen, <u>Performing Arts; The Economic Dilemma,</u> pages 557-560; Burgard, <u>Arts in the City,</u> pages 95-97, 113-117, 147-149; and Toffler, <u>The Culture Consumers</u>, pages 243-247.

National Endowment for the Arts. <u>Arts Library Acquisitions</u> <u>List.</u> Monthly. Washington, D. C.

Prieve, E. Arthur, and Ira W. Allen. <u>Administration in the</u> <u>Arts: An Annotated Bibliography of Selected References.</u> Madison: University of Wisconsin, Graduate School of Business, Center for Arts Administration, 1973. 111p.

Quint, Barbara and Lois Newman. "Performing Arts Centers and Economic Aspects of the Performing Arts: A Selective Bibliography." Santa Monica, Calif.: Rand Corp., 1969. 13p.

Schoolcraft, Ralph Newman. <u>Performing Arts/Books in Print:</u> <u>An Annotated Bibliography.</u> New York: Drama Book Specialists, 1973. 761p.

Whalon, Marion K. <u>Performing Arts Research: A Guide to</u> <u>Information Sources.</u> Detroit: Gale Research, 1976. 280p.

See Associations, Councils, and Other Organizations, (next page) for addresses to write to request lists of publications.

It is also noted that many of the books listed throughout the present work include excellent bibliographies: for example, Baumol and Bowen, <u>Performing Arts; The Economic Dilemma,</u> pages 557-560; Burgard, <u>Arts in the City,</u> pages 95-97, 113-117, 147-149; and Toffler, <u>The Culture Consumers,</u> pages 243-247.

ASSOCIATIONS, COUNCILS,
AND OTHER ORGANIZATIONS

Advocates for the Arts
570 Seventh Avenue, 17th Floor
New York, New York 10018
John Hightower, Chairman

> This is a program of the American Councils of the Arts,
> designed to encourage citizens' action for the arts, par-
> ticularly in support of the legal rights and economic
> security of creative artists. It offers legal advice to
> artists in the areas of copyright, censorship, taxes, et
> al.

> Publications: Arts Advocate, quarterly.

American Association of Museums
1055 Thomas Jefferson Street, NW
Suite 428
Washington, D. C. 20007
Dr. Richard McLanathan, Director
Membership: 6400

> This organization represents museums on the national
> level; sponsors seminars, training courses, and annual
> conferences; maintains advisory and placement services;
> offers administrative and technical assistance; collects
> and reports vital statistics on museums.

> Publications: Aviso (newsletter), monthly; Museum
> News, six issues per year; The Official Museum Dir-
> ectory, biennial; other special reports and books.

American Council for the Arts
570 Seventh Avenue, 17th Floor
New York, New York 10018
Michael Newton, President
Membership: 910

This association of municipal, community and state arts councils, as well as of community leaders and national arts organizations, serves as a central source of information and assistance. It conducts an extensive arts research program and plans workshops and seminars.

Publications: ACA Report, monthly; ACA Word from Washington, monthly; many useful reference tools and impressive studies. Write for the Current ACA publications list.

American Federation of Arts
41 East 56th Street
New York, New York 10021
Wilder Green, Director
Membership: 3000

This membership of art institutions and individuals sponsors art appreciation in the United States, particularly in localities without extensive artistic opportunities. It also seeks to foster better international understanding through the exchange of arts. It offers art critics' workshops, seminars, and other special programs and advisory services.

Publications: Exhibition catalogs and reference books on film as art.

American Music Center
250 West 57th Street
Suite 626-7
New York, New York 10019
Mrs. Margaret Jory, Executive Director
Membership: 950

The American Music Center maintains a library and information center for serious American music. Included are scores, tapes and records, as well as extensive biographical information on American performers and composers.

Publications: Newsletter, six times per year.

American Music Conference
1000 Skokie Boulevard
Wilmette, Illinois 60091
Leslie B. Propp, President

This organization is supported by the music industry and independent music firms and educators as their public service organization.

Publications: Music USA (annual review of the music industry); other booklets and pamphlets.

American Symphony Orchestra League
Symphony Hill, P. O. Box 669
Vienna, Virginia 22180
Ralph Black, Executive Director
Membership: 3200

The League serves as a clearinghouse and coordinating agency for all matters pertaining to symphony orchestras. Training programs, workshops, an annual conference, job counseling services, administrative assistance and research are among its activities.

Publications: Symphony News, bimonthly; bulletins, manuals and reports.

Association of American Dance Companies
162 West 56th Street,
New York, New York 10019
John N. Gingrich, President
Membership: 800

The functions of the Association of American Dance Companies are to bring American dance companies together to learn from each other, to provide information to government and private funding sources on behalf of the companies, to save money for the companies by using combined purchasing power, and to provide management assistance, job placement assistance, and statistical comparisons. Members are professional and non-professional nonprofit performing dance companies.

Publications: AADC Newsletter, quarterly; bulletins and announcements of special publications.

Association of College, University and Community Arts Administrators
P. O. Box 2137
Madison, Wisconsin 53701
William Dawson, Executive Director
Membership: 700

This is a professional association of colleges, universities, nonprofit and community arts organizations involved in the presentation of the performing arts. Its services include an annual booking conference, workshops on management techniques for performing arts, and contracts negotiations.

Publications: Bulletin and Event Report, monthly; pamphlets and reports.

Business Committee for the Arts
1700 Broadway
New York, New York 10019
G. A. McLellan, President
Membership: 125

Membership is by invitation, with an effort made to maintain representation by type of business or industry and by geographical location. The purpose of the Committee is to encourage sponsorship of the arts by business, to provide information to corporations wanting to initiate arts programs, and to represent business in cooperative efforts with the government or private agencies.

This need for increased business involvement with the arts was outlined in the 1965 Rockefeller Panel Report. In September of 1966, the idea of the committee was proposed by David Rockefeller, President of the Chase Manhattan Bank, in a speech to the National Industrial Conference Board.

Publications: BCA News and Arts Business, monthly newsletters, plus many pamphlets, all gratis; various books, such as The New Patrons of the Arts (Abrams, 1973), written by Gideon Chagy, with prices available on request.

Central Opera Service
Metropolitan Opera, Lincoln Center
New York, New York 10023
Maria F. Rich, Administrative Director
Membership: 1150

The purpose of this association is to foster closer association among opera companies and opera workshops, and to serve as an information clearinghouse for the operatic field. Its members include opera companies, university and college opera workshops and music departments, artists active in the operatic field, opera company board members, foundations active in the arts, state art agencies, and public and university libraries.

Committee on Research in Dance
35 West Fourth Street
Room 675
New York University Department of Dance Education
New York, New York   10003
Membership: 1000

This group includes dance instructors, administrators of dance departments in colleges, universities and professional institutions, and those conducting dance-related research.   Its aim is to encourage dance research and to develop a list of resources on dance by geographical and subject areas.

Publications: Dance Research Annual; Dance Research Journal, semi-annual.

Council on Foundations
888 Seventh Avenue
New York, New York   10019
David F. Freeman, President
Membership: 840

The Council on Foundations is a nonprofit membership organization which provides a wide range of advisory and consulting services to its members and to the grant-making field.

Publications: Foundation News, bimonthly; Annual Report; Community Foundation News, irregular; Regional Reporter, irregular; pamphlets and books.

The Foundation Center
888 Seventh Avenue
New York, New York   10019
Thomas R. Buckman, President

The Foundation Center was incorporated in 1956 and is supported by over 200 sponsoring foundations.   Its three main functions are to provide information, conduct research, and publish relevant material in the field.

It maintains three national collections of source materials in New York, Washington, D. C. , and Chicago, in addition to over 60 regional collections in public or university and college libraries throughout the United States.

Publications: The Foundation Directory, irregular; Foundation Grants Index, annual; Foundation Grants to Individuals; About Foundations; Foundation Center Source Book Profiles; Foundation Center National Data Book; International Philanthropy.

Foundation for the Extension and Development of the American Professional Theatre
1500 Broadway
New York, New York 10036
Frederic B. Vogel, Executive Director

FEDAPT is a not-for-profit service agency offering counseling in arts management to professional theatre projects throughout the United States. Its purpose is to develop, strengthen and improve the administrative and managerial capabilities of both emergent and existing theatre operations.

Publications: Subscription Guidelines; Box Office Guidelines; Investigation Guidelines for Setting Up a Theatre; other informative monographs.

International Council of Museums
Maison de l'Unesco
F-75015
Paris, France
Luis Monreal, Secretary General
Membership: 5700

This professional organization, open to all members of the museum profession, was set up to further international cooperation among museums.

Publications: COM News, quarterly; International Museological Bibliography, annual.

International Society of Performing Arts Administrators
615 Louisiana
Houston, Texas 77002
James Bernhard, Secretary
Membership: 175

Open to sales agents, artists' managers and persons or
organizations who manage and promote professional con-
certs, the ISPAA seeks to promote interest and appreciation in the performing arts.

Publications: Bulletin, nine times per year; Membership Directory, annual.

Lincoln Center for the Performing Arts
1865 Broadway
New York, New York 10023
John W. Mazzola, President

Lincoln Center is a cultural community of arts and artists to promote and encourage musical and performing
arts. Its educational institutions include the Juillard
School, committed to high quality professional training,
and the New York Public Library at Lincoln Center (Library and Museum of the Performing Arts). The performing institutions are the New York Philharmonic Symphony Society, the Metropolitan Opera Association, and
the New York City Center of Music and Drama, which
is responsible for the New York City Ballet and the New
York City Opera.

Metropolitan Opera Guild
1865 Broadway
New York, New York 10023
Dario Soria, Managing Director
Membership: 100, 000

This organization promotes interest in opera, furthers
musical education, and broadens support for the Metropolitan Opera. It also maintains a library of libretti,
a vocal score service, and a mail-order service for
books and records.

Publications: Opera News, weekly during December-
April, monthly from May-November.

National Association for Regional Ballet
1860 Broadway
New York, New York 10023
Doris Hering, Executive Director
Membership: 120

Composed of companies affiliated with one of the five

regional ballet associations in the United States and Canada, this association sponsors ballet festivals and conferences on choreography, publishes literature on regional ballet, and works to enhance the recognition of regional ballet companies.

Publications: Dance/America (newsletter), quarterly.

National Council on Philanthropy
680 Fifth Avenue
New York, New York 10019
Oscar C. Carr, President and Chief Executive Officer

The National Council on Philanthropy is a unique nonprofit organization dedicated to strengthening and en-
riching private resources to better meet public needs.
With more than twenty years of service, the Council
provides the only national forum for representatives from
the broadest spectrum of service and educational insti-
tutions--corporations, foundations, charitable intermedi-
aries and tax experts on philanthropy--to work together
to improve the quality and scope of philanthropic efforts
in America and overseas.

Publications: International Business Philanthropy, edited
by Richard Eells.

National Foundation on the Arts and the Humanities
806 Fifteenth Street, N. W.
Washington, D. C.   20506

National Endowment for the Arts
Livingston Biddle, Chairman

National Endowment for the Humanities
Joseph Duffey, Chairman

The National Endowment for the Arts and the National
Endowment for the Humanities are sister agencies.
These two endowments are the primary components of
the National Foundation on the Arts and the Humanities,
a federal government agency established by Congress in
September 1965.   Each endowment has its own advisory
council.   The National Council on the Arts provides ad-
vice on policies, procedures, and grant applications
to the chairman of the National Endowment for the
Arts.

The National Endowment for the Arts' role is to aid and to encourage the Arts in America, primarily through grant-making of Congressionally appropriated funds. The Endowment makes grants both directly to artists and arts organizations across the country and indirectly, under the Federal-State Partnership Program, through funds made available to official State Arts Councils for use in their own states or regions.

Publications: Annual Report; Program Announcement (Write to the appropriate Endowment).

National Opera Association
c/o Constance Eberhart
823 Hotel Wellington
Seventh and 55th Streets
New York, New York 10019
Membership: 600

The National Opera Association is comprised of opera composers, conductors, directors, managers, and producers; operatic music publishers; librettists, teachers, translaters; opera companies; colleges, universities, schools of music, and workshops. Its purpose is to advance the appreciation, composition and publication on opera.

Publications: Opera Journal, quarterly; Membership Directory, annual; addresses, papers, reports and manuals.

National Society of Fund Raisers
1511 K Street, NW
Suite 831
Washington, D. C. 20005
Fletcher R. Hall, CAE, President
Membership: 1500

Members are individuals, not companies or organizations. They are engaged in fund-raising programs for non-profit organizations in education, health, welfare and religion. Research and instruction in the field of fund-raising are sponsored. Workshops and seminars are offered periodically.

Publications: Newsletter, 11 times a year; Directory of National Membership, annual; Journal of Fund Raising, annual.

Publishing Center for Cultural Resources
27 West 53rd Street
New York, New York   10019
M. J. Gladstone, Director

>The Publishing Center is a nonprofit corporation crea-
>ted to help nonprofit educational organizations throughout
>the United States achieve economical and effective pub-
>lication.   The Center assists in any aspect of publishing
>which such organizations cannot perform themselves be-
>cause they lack manpower, skills, space or equipment.

Rockefeller Brothers Fund
30 Rockefeller Plaza
New York, New York   10020
Laurence S. Rockefeller, Chairman

>Grants are made to nonprofit organizations under three
>programs--New York City, national, and international--
>to support a variety of interests, including the visual
>and performing arts.   This foundation sponsored a land-
>mark study in this field, The Performing Arts: Prob-
>lems and Prospects; Rockefeller Panel Report on the
>Future of Theatre, Dance, Music in America (McGraw-
>Hill, 1965).

Theatre Communications Group
355 Lexington Avenue
New York, New York   10017
Peter Zeisler, Director

>Not a membership organization, the Theatre Communica-
>tions Group is supported by grants to raise standards
>and aid in developing non-profit professional theatre.   It
>provides a casting information service, sponsors student
>auditions nationally, offers observership programs, of-
>fers a subscription consultant, compiles statistics,
>maintains director files, personnel referral program,
>and theatre resource files.

>Publications: Newsletter, monthly; Theatre Directory,
>annual; Subscribe Now! by Danny Newman (a reference
>book for audience-building through dynamic subscription
>techniques).

See the Encyclopedia of Associations, 11th Edition, Gale Research Company, 1977, three volumes. Volume I lists and fully describes nearly 16, 000 associations and professional societies. Sections 5 and 6 on "Educational and Cultural Organizations, " pages 429-632, cite many which are of special interest in Arts Administration.

See also The Foundation Directory, 6th edition, prepared by the Foundation Center and distributed by the Columbia University Press.

PUBLISHERS' ADDRESSES

AG PRESS. 1207 Moro Street, Manhattan, Kan. 66502.

ABINGDON PRESS. 201 Eighth Avenue South, Nashville, Tenn. 37202.

HARRY N. ABRAMS. 110 East 59th Street, New York, N.Y. 10022.

ACADEMIC MEDIA. 4300 West 62nd Street, Indianapolis, Ind. 46268.

ADELPHI UNIVERSITY PRESS. South Avenue, Garden City, N.Y. 11530.

ADVISORY COMMISSION ON FINANCING THE ARTS IN ILLI-NOIS. Room 2000, 160 North La Salle Street, Chicago, Ill. 60601.

ADVOCATES FOR THE ARTS. 570 Seventh Avenue, New York, N.Y. 10018.

ALLYN & BACON. 470 Atlantic Avenue, Boston, Mass. 02210.

AMACOM see AMERICAN MANAGEMENT ASSOCIATION

AMERICAN ACADEMY OF POLITICAL AND SOCIAL SCIENCES. 3937 Chestnut Street, Philadelphia, Pa. 19104.

AMERICAN ASSOCIATION FOR STATE AND LOCAL HISTORY. 1400 Eighth Avenue South, Nashville, Tenn. 37203.

AMERICAN ASSOCIATION OF FUND RAISING COUNSEL. 500 Fifth Avenue, New York, N.Y. 10036.

AMERICAN ASSOCIATION OF MUSEUMS. 2233 Wisconsin Avenue, N.W., Washington, D.C. 20007.

AMERICAN COLLEGE PUBLIC RELATIONS ASSOCIATION
see CASE

AMERICAN COUNCIL FOR THE ARTS IN EDUCATION. 18
East 48th Street, New York, N. Y. 10017.

AMERICAN CRAFTS COUNCIL. 44 West 53rd Street, New
York, N. Y. 10019.

AMERICAN EDUCATIONAL THEATRE ASSOCIATION. John
F. Kennedy Center for the Performing Arts, 726 Jackson Place, N. W. , Washington, D. C. 20566.

AMERICAN ELSEVIER see ELSEVIER-NORTH HOLLAND

AMERICAN INSTITUTE OF ARCHITECTS. 1735 New York
Avenue, N. W. , Washington, D. C. 20006.

AMERICAN INSTITUTE OF CERTIFIED PUBLIC ACCOUNT-
ANTS. 1211 Avenue of the Americas, New York, N. Y.
10036.

AMERICAN MANAGEMENT ASSOCIATION. 135 West 50th
Street, New York, N. Y. 10020.

AMERICAN THEATRE ASSOCIATION. 1317 "F" Street, N. W. ,
Washington, D. C. 20004.

ANNA PUBLISHING. 500 St. Andrews Boulevard, Winter
Park, Florida 32792.

ARCO PUB. CO. 219 Park Avenue South, New York, N. Y.
10003.

ARNO PRESS. 3 Park Avenue, New York, N. Y. 10017.

ART IN AMERICA. 150 East 58th Street, New York, N. Y.
10022.

ART SALES INDEX. Pond House, Weybridge, Surrey, Kent
13, England.

ARTS ADMINISTRATION RESEARCH INSTITUTE. 75 Sparks
Street, Cambridge, Mass. 02138.

ARTS COUNCIL OF GREAT BRITAIN. 105 Piccadilly, London WIV OAU, England.

ARTS COUNCILS OF AMERICA see ASSOCIATED COUNCILS OF THE ARTS

ARTS IN SOCIETY. University of Wisconsin-Madison, Room 728 Lowell Hall, 610 Langdon Street, Madison, Wis. 53706.

ASSOCIATED COUNCILS OF THE ARTS. 1564 Broadway, Room 820, New York, N. Y. 10036.

ASSOCIATION OF AMERICAN DANCE COMPANIES. 162 West 56th Street, New York, N. Y. 10019.

ASSOCIATION OF ART MUSEUM DIRECTORS. One East 70th Street, New York, N. Y. 10021.

ASSOCIATION OF COLLEGE AND UNIVERSITY CONCERT MANAGERS see ASSOCIATION OF COLLEGE, UNIVERSITY AND COMMUNITY ARTS ADMINISTRATORS

ASSOCIATION OF COLLEGE, UNIVERSITY AND COMMUNITY ARTS ADMINISTRATORS. P. O. Box 2137, Madison, Wis. 53701.

ASSOCIATION OF VOLUNTARY ACTION SCHOLARS. Box G-55, Boston College, Chestnut Hill, Mass. 02167.

ASSOCIATION PRESS. 291 Broadway, New York, N. Y. 10007.

ATHENEUM. Distributed by Book Warehouse, Inc. Vreeland Avenue, Boro of Totowa, Paterson, N. J. 07512.

AWARD BOOKS see UNIVERSAL PUBLISHING & DISTRIBUTING CORPORATION

AYER PRESS. West Washington Square, Philadelphia, Pa. 19106.

BALLANTINE BOOKS distributed by RANDOM HOUSE

A. S. BARNES. P. O. Box 421, Cranbury, N. J. 08512.

BASIC BOOKS. P. O. Box 4000, Scranton, Pa. 18501.

BAY AREA LAWYERS FOR THE ARTS. 25 Taylor Street, San Francisco, Calif. 94102.

BAY AREA SOCIAL RESPONSIBILITIES ROUND TABLE.   2745 Stuart # 3, Berkeley, Calif.   94705.

BEACON PRESS.   25 Beacon Street, Boston, Mass.   02108.

MATTHEW BENDER.   235 East 45th Street, New York, N. Y. 10017.

BERKLEE PRESS.   1140 Boylston Street, Boston, Mass. 02115.

BEVERLY HILLS BAR ASSOCIATION.   300 Beverly Drive, Beverly Hills, Calif.   90212.

BILLBOARD PUBLICATIONS. see   WATSON-GUPTILL

JOHN BLAIR.   1406 Plaza Drive, Winston-Salem, N. C. 27103.

BENJAMIN BLOM   see   ARNO PRESS

CLARK BOARDMAN.   435 Hudson Street, New York, N. Y. 10014.

R. R. BOWKER CO.   P. O. Box 1807, Ann Arbor, Mich. 48106.

GEORGE BRAZILLER.   One Park Avenue, New York, N. Y. 10016.

BROADCASTING PUBLICATIONS.   1735 DeSales Street, N. W. , Washington, D. C.   20036.

BROOKINGS INSTITUTION.   1775 Massachusetts Avenue, N. W. , Washington, D. C.   20036.

BROOKLYN MUSEUM.   188 Eastern Parkway, Brooklyn, N. Y. 11238.

BUSINESS COMMITTEE FOR THE ARTS.   1700 Broadway, Fifth Floor, New York, N. Y.   10019.

CALIFORNIA ARTS COMMISSION.   Document Section, Department of General Services.   P. O. Box 1612, Sacramento, Calif.   95802.

CANADIAN CONFERENCE OF THE ARTS.   3 Church Street, Suite 47, Toronto, Ontario, MEE IMZ, Canada.

CASE (Council for Advancement and Support of Education). One Dupont Circle, Suite 600, Washington, D. C. 20036.

CENTER FOR THE STUDY OF DEMOCRATIC INSTITUTIONS. Box 4068, 2056 Eucalyptus Hill Road, Santa Barbara, Calif. 93103.

CHILTON BOOK CO. 201 King of Prussia Road, Radnor, Pa. 19089.

CLARENDON PRESS see OXFORD UNIVERSITY PRESS, INC.

CLEVELAND AREA ARTS COUNCIL. 510 The Arcade, Cleveland, Ohio 44114.

COLUMBIA UNIVERSITY PRESS. 136 S. Broadway, Irvington-on-Hudson, N. Y. 10533.

COMMERCE CLEARING HOUSE. 1220 Avenue of the Americas, New York, N. Y. 10036.

COMMISSION ON PRIVATE PHILANTHROPY AND PUBLIC NEEDS. c/o John Filer, Aetna Life & Casualty, 15 Farmington Avenue, Hartford, Conn. 06115.

COMMITTEE FOR ECONOMIC DEVELOPMENT. 477 Madison Avenue, New York, N. Y. 10022.

CONFERENCE BOARD. 845 Third Avenue, New York, N. Y. 10022.

CONTEMPORARY BOOKS (formerly Henry Regnery). 180 N. Michigan Avenue, Chicago, Ill. 60601.

CONTINUING EDUCATION PUBLICATIONS. P. O. Box 2590, Station A, Champaign, Ill. 61820.

CORNELL UNIVERSITY PRESS. 124 Roberts Place, Ithaca, N. Y. 14850.

COUNCIL FOR FINANCIAL AID TO EDUCATION. 680 Fifth Avenue, New York, N. Y. 10019.

COUNCIL OF PLANNING LIBRARIANS. P. O. Box 229, Monticello, Ill. 61856.

COUNCIL ON FOUNDATIONS. 888 Seventh Avenue, New York, N. Y. 10019.

COWARD, McCANN, AND GEOGHAGEN. 390 Murray Hill Parkway, East Rutherford, N. J. 07073.

CRAFTS REPORT PUB. CO. 116 University Place, New York, N. Y. 10003.

CRANE, RUSSAK. 347 Madison Avenue, New York, N. Y. 10017.

THOMAS Y. CROWELL. 666 Fifth Avenue, New York, N. Y. 10019.

CROWELL-COLLIER EDUCATIONAL CORP. 866 Third Avenue, New York, N. Y. 10022.

CROWN PUBLISHERS. 419 Park Avenue South, New York, N. Y. 10016.

DBS see DRAMA BOOK SPECIALISTS

DAVID AND CHARLES. P. O. Box 57, North Pomfret, Vermont 05033.

WILLIAM DAWSON. Cannon House, Folkestone, Kent CT 19 5EE, England.

DEL CAPO PUBLICATIONS. West Melrose Building, Nashville, Tenn. 37204.

DELACORTE PRESS see DIAL PRESS

DEMBAR EDUCATIONAL RESEARCH SERVICES. Box 1605, Madison, Wis. 53701.

DES MOINES AREA COMMUNITY COLLEGE. 2006 South Ankeny Boulevard, Ankeny, Iowa. 50317.

DIAL PRESS. One Dag Hammarskjold Plaza, 245 East 47th Street, New York, N. Y. 10017.

DODD, MEAD. 79 Madison Avenue, New York, N. Y. 10016.

DOUBLEDAY. 501 Franklin Avenue, Garden City, N. Y. 11530.

DOUGLAS BOOK CORP. see WORLD PUB. CO.

DRAMA BOOK SPECIALISTS. 150 West 52nd Street, New York, N. Y. 10019.

DRYDEN ASSOCIATES. Dryden, N. Y. 13053.

DUKE UNIVERSITY PRESS. Box 6697 College Station, Durham, N. C. 27708.

E. P. DUTTON. 2 Park Avenue, New York, N. Y. 10016.

EDITIONS PUBLISOL. Gracie Station, New York, N. Y. 10028.

EDITIONS TECHNIQUES ET ECONOMIQUES. 3r Soufflot 5e, St. Etienne, France.

LARRY EDMONDS. 6658 Hollywood Boulevard, Los Angeles, Calif. 90028.

EDUCATIONAL FACILITIES LABORATORIES. 850 Third Avenue, New York, N. Y. 10022.

ELSEVIER-NORTH HOLLAND PUB. CO. 52 Vanderbilt Avenue, New York, N. Y. 10017.

PAUL S. ERIKSSON. Distributed by Independent Publishers Group, 14 Vanderbenter Avenue, Port Washington, N. Y. 11050.

M. EVANS & CO. 216 East 49th Street, New York, N. Y. 10017.

FAMILY SERVICE ASSOCIATION OF AMERICA. 44 East 23rd Street, New York, N. Y. 10010.

FARRAR, STRAUS, AND GIROUX, INC. 19 Union Square, West, New York, N. Y. 10003.

FEDERAL LEGAL PUBLICATIONS. 95 Morton Street, New York, N. Y. 10014.

FEDERAL RESERVE BANK OF PHILADELPHIA. 925 Chestnut Street, Philadelphia, Pa. 19101.

FICTION COLLECTIVE. c/o Brooklyn College (CUNY), Department of English, Brooklyn, N. Y. 11201.

THE 501 (c) (3) GROUP. Suite 600, One Dupont Circle, Washington, D. C. 20036.

FOCAL PRESS. 31 Fitzroy Square, London WIP 6BH, England.

FOLLETT PUB. CO. 1010 West Washington Boulevard, Chicago, Ill. 60607.

FORD FOUNDATION. 320 East 43rd Street, New York, N. Y. 10017.

FORDHAM UNIVERSITY PRESS. University Box L, Bronx, N. Y. 10458.

FORT WAYNE FINE ARTS FOUNDATION. 324 Penn Avenue, Fort Wayne, Ind. 46805.

THE FOUNDATION CENTER. 888 Seventh Avenue, New York, N. Y. 10019.

FOUNDATION FOR THE COMMUNITY OF ARTISTS. 220 Fifth Avenue, New York, N. Y. 10001.

FOUNDATION FOR THE EXTENSION AND DEVELOPMENT OF THE AMERICAN PROFESSIONAL THEATRE. 1500 Broadway, New York, N. Y. 10036.

FOUNDATION PRESS. 170 Old Country Road, Mineola, N. Y. 11501.

FRANKLIN AND MARSHALL COLLEGE. Lancaster, Pa. 17604.

FREE PRESS distributed by MACMILLAN

FUND RAISING MANAGEMENT. 224 Seventh Street, Garden City, N. Y. 11530.

FUNK & WAGNALLS distributed by THOMAS Y. CROWELL

G/L TAB BOOKS see TAB BOOKS

GALE RESEARCH CO. Book Tower, Detroit, Mich. 48226.

GEE TEE BEE. 11901 Sunset Boulevard, No. 102, Los Angeles, Calif. 90049.

GLIDE PUBLICATIONS. 330 Ellis Street, San Francisco, Calif. 94102.

GOLDEN PRESS see WESTERN PUB. CO.

GRANTSMANSHIP CENTER. 1015 West Olympic Boulevard, Los Angeles, Calif. 90015.

GROSSET & DUNLAP. 51 Madison Avenue, New York, N. Y. 10010.

HANDEL & CO. 2720 Stemmons Freeway, Suite 510, South Building, Dallas, Texas 75201.

HARCOURT BRACE AND WORLD see next entry

HARCOURT BRACE JOVANOVICH. 757 Third Avenue, New York, N. Y. 10017.

HARMONY BOOKS. Distributed by Crown Publications, Inc. One Park Avenue, New York, N. Y. 10016.

HARPER & ROW. Scranton, Pa. 18512.

HARVARD UNIVERSITY PRESS. 79 Garden Street, Cambridge, Mass. 02138.

ARNOLD HARVEY ASSOCIATES. P. O. Box 89, Commack, New York, N. Y. 11725.

HASTINGS HOUSE. 10 East 40th Street, New York, N. Y. 10016.

HAWTHORN BOOKS. 260 Madison Avenue, New York, N. Y. 10016.

D. C. HEATH. 125 Spring Street, Lexington, Mass. 02173.

HILL AND WANG. 19 Union Square West, New York, N. Y. 10003.

HOBBS, DORMAN. 441 Lexington Avenue, New York, N. Y. 10017.

HOFSTRA UNIVERSITY. 1000 Fulton Avenue, Hempstead, N. Y. 11550.

HOLT, RINEHART & WINSTON. 383 Madison Avenue, New York, N. Y. 10017.

HOUGHTON MIFFLIN. 2 Park Street, Boston, Mass. 02107.

HUMANITIES PRESS. Atlantic Highlands, N. J. 07716.

INDIANA UNIVERSITY PRESS. Tenth and Morton Streets, Bloomington, Ind. 47401.

INFORMATION CANADA. 171 Slater Street, Ottawa, Canada K1A OS9.

INTERCOLLEGIATE CASE CLEARING HOUSE. Soldiers Field Post Office, Boston, Mass. 02163.

INTERSTATE PRINTERS & PUBLISHERS. 19 North Jackson Street, Danville, Ill. 61832.

RICHARD D. IRWIN. 1818 Ridge Road, Homewood, Ill. 60430.

JDR 3rd FUND. 50 Rockefeller Plaza, New York, N. Y. 10020.

JOINT COMMITTEE ON CULTURAL RESOURCES. David Cwi, Johns Hopkins University, Center for Metropolitan Planning and Research, Baltimore, Maryland 21218.

JOURNAL OF TAXATION. 125 East 56th Street, New York, N. Y. 10022.

ALFRED A. KNOPF distributed by RANDOM HOUSE

KRAUS-THOMSON ORGANIZATION. Route 100, Millwood, N. Y. 10546.

KUNST & TECHNIK. 8 Lipowskystrasse, Munich 70, West Germany.

LAW-ARTS PUBLISHERS. 453 Greenwich Street, New York, N. Y. 10013.

LEARNING RESOURCES CORP. 7594 Eads Avenue, La Jolla, Calif. 92037.

LEXINGTON BOOKS see D. C. HEATH

LIEBER-ATHERTON. 1841 Broadway, New York, N. Y. 10023.

LITTLE, BROWN. 200 West Street, Waltham, Mass. 02154.

LIVERIGHT PUB. CORP. see W. W. NORTON

LOND PUBLICATIONS. Pomona, N. Y. 10970.

LOS ANGELES COUNTY MUSEUM OF ART. 5905 Wilshire Boulevard, Los Angeles, Calif. 90036.

LOS ANGELES DANCE THEATRE. 1892 El Cerrito Place, Los Angeles, Calif. 90068.

LUTHERAN SOCIAL SERVICES OF MINNESOTA. 2414 Park Avenue, Minneapolis, Minn. 55404.

M. I. T. PRESS. 28 Carleton Street, Cambridge, Mass. 02142.

McGRAW-HILL. 1221 Avenue of the Americas, New York, N. Y. 10036.

DAVID McKAY. 750 Third Avenue, New York, N. Y. 10017.

MACMILLAN. Riverside, N. J. 08075.

MARKETING SCIENCE INSTITUTE. 14 Story Street, Cambridge, Mass. 02138.

MAYFIELD PUB. CO. 285 Hamilton Avenue, Palo Alto, Calif. 94301.

METROPOLITAN CULTURAL ALLIANCE. 37 Newbury Street, Boston, Mass. 02159.

MICHIGAN STATE UNIVERSITY PRESS. Manly Miles Building, 1405 South Harrison Road, East Lansing, Mich. 48824.

WILLIAM MORROW. Wilmore Warehouse, 6 Henderson Drive, West Caldwell, N. J. 07706.

MUSIC EDUCATORS NATIONAL CONFERENCE. 1902 Association Drive, Reston, Va. 22091.

MUSIC INDUSTRY COUNCIL. c/o J. W. Pepper and Son, Inc. , Box 850, Valley Forge, Pa. 19482.

MUSIC INFORMATION SERVICE. 310 Madison Avenue, New York, N. Y. 10017.

NTL LEARNING RESOURCES CORP. 2817-N Door Avenue, Fairfax, Va. 22030.

NASH PUB. CO. distributed by E. P. DUTTON

NATIONAL BUREAU OF ECONOMIC RESEARCH. 261 Madison Avenue, New York, N. Y. 10016.

NATIONAL CATHOLIC DEVELOPMENT CONFERENCE. 119 North Park Avenue, Rockville Centre, N. Y. 11570.

NATIONAL CENTER FOR VOLUNTARY ACTION. 1785 Massachusetts Avenue, N. W., Washington, D. C. 20036.

NATIONAL COMMITTEE FOR CULTURAL RESOURCES. 11th Floor, 1865 Broadway, New York, N. Y. 10023.

NATIONAL COUNCIL OF YOUNG MEN'S CHRISTIAN ASSOCIATIONS. 291 Broadway, New York, N. Y. 10007.

NATIONAL ENDOWMENT FOR THE ARTS. 806 Fifteenth Street, N. W., Washington, D. C. 20506.

NATIONAL ENDOWMENT FOR THE HUMANITIES. 806 Fifteenth Street, N. W., Washington, D. C. 20506.

NATIONAL PRESS BOOKS see MAYFIELD PUB. CO.

NATIONAL RESEARCH CENTER OF THE ARTS. 1270 Avenue of the Americas, New York, N. Y. 10020.

NATIONAL TAX ASSOCIATION--TAX INSTITUTE OF AMERICA. 21 East State Street, Columbus, Ohio 43215.

NELSON-HALL. 325 West Jackson Boulevard, Chicago, Ill. 60606.

NEW YORK CITY MAYOR'S COMMITTEE ON CULTURAL POLICY distributed by PUBLISHING CENTER FOR CULTURAL RESOURCES

NEW YORK CITY MAYOR'S OFFICE FOR VOLUNTEERS. 51 Chambers, New York, N. Y. 10007.

NEW YORK FOUNDATION FOR THE ARTS distributed by PUBLISHING CENTER FOR CULTURAL RESOURCES

NEW YORK GRAPHIC SOCIETY. 11 Beacon Street, Boston, Mass. 02108.

NEW YORK STATE ASSOCIATION OF MUSEUMS distributed by PUBLISHING CENTER FOR CULTURAL RESOURCES

NEW YORK STATE COLLEGE OF AGRICULTURE AND LIFE SCIENCES, Department of Communication Arts, Cornell University. Ithaca, N. Y. 14850

NEW YORK STATE COMMISSION ON CULTURAL RESOURCES. Governor A. E. Smith State Office Building, Albany, N. Y. 12225.

NEW YORK STATE COUNCIL ON THE ARTS. 250 West 57th Street, New York, N. Y. 10019.

NEW YORK STATE SCHOOL OF INDUSTRIAL AND LABOR RELATIONS. Box 1000, Cornell University, Ithaca, N. Y. 14853.

NEW YORK UNIVERSITY, Graduate School of Business Administration, Institute of Finance. 100 Trinity Place, New York, N. Y. 10006.

NEW YORK UNIVERSITY PRESS. 21 West Fourth Street, New York, N. Y. 10012.

NORTHWESTERN UNIVERSITY PRESS. 1735 Benson Avenue, Evanston, Ill. 60201.

W. W. NORTON. 500 Fifth Avenue, New York, N. Y. 10036.

OCEANA PUBLICATIONS. 75 Main Street, Dobbs Ferry, N. Y. 10522.

OCTOPUS BOOKS. 59 Grosvenor Street, London WIX 9DA, England.

OHIO UNIVERSITY PRESS. Scott Quadrangle, Athens, Ohio 45701.

OVERLOOK PRESS distributed by VIKING PRESS

OXFORD UNIVERSITY PRESS. 16-00 Pollitt Drive, Fair Lawn, N. J. 07410.

PACIFIC BOOKS. Box 558, Palo Alto, Calif. 94302.

PACIFIC NORTHWEST BALLET ASSOCIATION. 305 Harrison Street, Seattle, Wash. 98109.

PERFORMING ARTS ASSOCIATION OF NEW YORK. 245 West 52nd Street, New York, N. Y. 10019.

PILGRIM PRESS. 1505 Race Street, Philadelphia, Pa. 19102.

PILOT BOOKS. 347 5th Avenue, New York, N. Y. 10016.

PITMAN PUB. CORP. 6 Davis Drive, Belmont, Calif. 94002.

PLAYBOY PRESS distributed by SIMON & SCHUSTER

PLENUM PUB. CORP. 227 West 17th Street, New York, N. Y. 10011.

POCKET BOOKS see SIMON & SCHUSTER

PRACTISING LAW INSTITUTE. 810 Seventh Avenue, New York, N. Y. 10019.

PRAEGER see HOLT, RINEHART AND WINSTON

PRENTICE-HALL. Englewood Cliffs, N. J. 07632.

PRESENTATION PRESS. P. O. Box 2335, Middle City Station, Philadelphia, Pa. 19103.

PRICE WATERHOUSE. 60 Broad Street, New York, N. Y. 10004.

PRINCE PUBLISHERS. 349 East Northfield Road, Livingston, N. J. 07039.

PRINCETON UNIVERSITY PRESS. 41 William Street, Princeton, N. J. 08540.

PUBLIC AFFAIRS INFORMATION SERVICE. 11 West 40th Street, New York, N. Y. 10018.

PUBLIC AFFAIRS PRESS. 419 New Jersey Avenue, S. E. , Washington, D. C. 20003.

PUBLIC SERVICE MATERIALS CENTER. 355 Lexington Avenue, New York, N. Y. 10017.

PUBLISHING CENTER FOR CULTURAL RESOURCES. 27
West 53rd Street, New York, N. Y. 10019.

G. P. PUTNAM. 390 Murray Hill Parkway, East Rutherford,
N. J. 07073.

QUEEN ANNE PRESS. 12 Vandy Street, London E. C. 2,
England.

QUIGLEY PUBLICATIONS. 1270 Avenue of the Americas,
New York, N. Y. 10020.

RAND CORP. 1700 Main Street, Santa Monica, Calif. 90406.

RANDOM HOUSE. 457 Hahn Road, Westminster, Md. 21157.

HENRY REGNERY see CONTEMPORARY BOOKS

RENAISSANCE EDITIONS. 527 Madison Avenue, New York,
N. Y. 10022.

RICHARDS ROSEN PRESS. 29 East 21st Street, New York,
N. Y. 10010.

F. B. ROTHMAN AND CO. 57 Leuning Street, South Hackensack, N. J. 07606.

ROTTERDAM UNIVERSITY PRESS distributed by HUMANI-
TIES PRESS

RUTGERS UNIVERSITY PRESS. 30 College Avenue, New
Brunswick, N. J. 08901.

RUSSELL SAGE FOUNDATION distributed by BASIC BOOKS

ST. MARTIN'S PRESS. 175 Fifth Avenue, New York, N. Y.
10010.

SAN MATEO FOUNDATION. 1204 Burlingame Avenue # 10,
Burlingame, Calif. 94010.

SAXON HOUSE distributed by ATHENEUM

SCARECROW PRESS. Box 656, Metuchen, N. J. 08840.

SCHENKMAN. 3 Mt. Auburn Place, Cambridge, Mass.
02138.

SCHOCKEN BOOKS. 200 Madison Avenue, New York, N. Y. 10016.

SCHOLARLY PRESS. 22929 Industrial Drive East, St. Clair Shores, Mich. 48080.

SCREEN ACTORS GUILD. 7750 West Sunset Boulevard, Hollywood, Calif. 90046.

SCRIBNER'S. Vreeland Avenue, Totowa, N. J. 07512.

SEABURY PRESS. Distributed by Seabury Service Center, Somers, Conn. 06071.

SEVEN ARTS PRESS. 6605 Hollywood Boulevard, No. 215, Hollywood, Calif. 90028.

SIMON & SCHUSTER. 1230 Avenue of the Americas, New York, N. Y. 10020.

ALFRED P. SLOAN FOUNDATION. 630 Fifth Avenue, New York, N. Y. 10020.

SMITHSONIAN INSTITUTION PRESS. Distributed by George Braziller, Inc. , P. O. Box 1641, Washington, D. C. 20013.

SPRING HILL CONFERENCE CENTER see PUBLISHING CENTER FOR CULTURAL RESOURCES

STATE UNIVERSITY OF NEW YORK PRESS. c/o Publisher's Marketing Group, P. O. Box 350, Momence, Ill. 60954.

STATISTICAL RESEARCH. Westfield, N. J. 07091.

STEIN & DAY. 122 East 42nd Street, Suite 3602, New York, N. Y. 10020.

LYLE STUART. 120 Enterprise Avenue, Secaucus, N. J. 07094.

SUPPORT CENTER/COMMUNITY MANAGER CENTER. 1424 16th Street, N. W. , Washington, D. C. 20036.

SWALLOW PRESS. 811 West Junior Terrace, Chicago, Ill. 60613.

TAB BOOKS. Monterey and Pinola Avenues, Blue Ridge Summit, Pa. 17214.

TAFT CORP. 1000 Vermont Avenue, N.W. , Washington, D.C. 20005.

TAFT PRODUCTS see TAFT CORP.

TAMARIND LITHOGRAPHY WORKSHOP. 1112 Tamarind, Los Angeles, Calif. 90038.

J. P. TARCHER. 9110 Sunset Boulevard, Los Angeles, Calif. 90069.

TARCHER/GOUSHA GUIDES see J. P. TARCHER

TAX INSTITUTE OF AMERICA see NATIONAL TAX AS-SOCIATION--TAX INSTITUTE OF AMERICA

TEMPLE UNIVERSITY, Bureau of Economic and Business Research, School of Business Administration. Philadelphia, Pa. 19122.

THEATRE COMMUNICATIONS GROUP. 355 Lexington Avenue, New York, N.Y. 10017.

CHARLES C. THOMAS. 301-327 East Lawrence Avenue, Springfield, Ill. 62717.

TWAYNE PUBLISHERS. c/o G. K. Hall, 70 Lincoln Street, Boston, Mass. 02111.

TWENTIETH CENTURY FUND. 41 East 70th Street, New York, N.Y. 10021.

UNESCO see UNIPUB

UNIPUB. Box 433 Murray Hill Station, New York, N.Y. 10016.

FREDERICK UNGAR. 250 Park Avenue South, New York, N.Y. 10003.

UNITED NATIONS Educational, Scientific, and Cultural Organization (UNESCO) see UNIPUB

U.S. BUREAU OF LABOR STATISTICS. 441 G Street, N.W. , Washington, D.C. 20212.

U. S. DEPARTMENT OF THE INTERIOR, NATIONAL PARK SERVICE   see   U. S. GOVERNMENT PRINTING OF- FICE

U. S. GOVERNMENT PRINTING OFFICE.   Washington, D. C. 20402.

U. S. OFFICE OF EDUCATION   see   U. S. GOVERNMENT PRINTING OFFICE

UNIVERSAL PUBLISHING AND DISTRIBUTING CORP.   350 Kennedy Drive, Hauppauge, New York   11788.

UNIVERSITY MICROFILMS.   300 North Zeeb Road, Ann Ar- bor, Mich.   48106.

UNIVERSITY OF ALABAMA PRESS.   Drawer 2877, Univer- sity, Alabama   35486.

UNIVERSITY OF CALIFORNIA BERKELEY, INSTITUTE OF GOVERNMENTAL STUDIES.   348 Library Annex, Uni- versity of California, Berkeley, Calif.   94720.

UNIVERSITY OF CALIFORNIA LOS ANGELES, GRADUATE SCHOOL OF MANAGEMENT.   405 Hilgard Avenue, Los Angeles, Calif.   90024.

UNIVERSITY OF CALIFORNIA LOS ANGELES, INSTITUTE OF INDUSTRIAL RELATIONS.   405 Hilgard Avenue, Los Angeles, Calif.   90024.

UNIVERSITY OF CALIFORNIA LOS ANGELES, LIBRARY. 405 Hilgard Avenue, Los Angeles, Calif.   90024.

UNIVERSITY OF CALIFORNIA PRESS.   2223 Fulton Street, Berkeley, Calif.   94720.

UNIVERSITY OF CHICAGO PRESS.   11030 South Langley Avenue, Chicago, Ill.   60628.

UNIVERSITY OF ILLINOIS PRESS.   Urbana, Ill.   61801.

UNIVERSITY OF KANSAS PRESS.   366 Watson Library, Law- rence, Kan.   66044.

UNIVERSITY OF MICHIGAN PRESS.   615 East University, Ann Arbor, Mich.   48106.

UNIVERSITY OF MINNESOTA PRESS. 2037 University Avenue South East, Minneapolis, Minn. 55455

UNIVERSITY OF SHEFFIELD see ARTS COUNCIL OF GREAT BRITAIN

UNIVERSITY OF SOUTHERN CALIFORNIA LAW CENTER. University Park, Los Angeles, Calif. 90007.

UNIVERSITY OF WISCONSIN ARTS COUNCIL. 807 West Dayton, Madison, Wis. 53715.

UNIVERSITY OF WISCONSIN, Graduate School of Business, Center for Arts Administration. Madison, Wis. 53706.

UNIVERSITY OF WISCONSIN PRESS. P. O. Box 1379, Madison, Wis. 53701.

UNIVERSITY OF WISCONSIN, UNIVERSITY EXTENSION. 606 State Street, Madison, Wis. 53706.

VAN NOSTRAND REINHOLD. Division of Litton Educational Publishing, Inc., 450 West 33rd Street, New York, N. Y. 10001.

VANGUARD PRESS. 424 Madison Avenue, New York, N. Y. 10017.

VANTAGE PRESS. 516 West 34th Street, New York, N. Y. 10001.

VARIETY. 154 West 46th Street, New York, N. Y. 10036.

VERLAG DOKUMENTATION SAUR KG. Distributed (Western Hemisphere) by R. R. BOWKER CO.

VIKING PRESS. 625 Madison Avenue, New York, N. Y. 10022.

MARIE VOGT. 5362 Main Street, Sylvania, Ohio 43560.

VOLUNTEER LAWYERS FOR THE ARTS. 36 West 44th Street, New York, N. Y. 10036.

VOLUNTEER MANAGEMENT ASSOCIATES. 279 South Cedar Brook Road, Boulder, Colo. 80302.

VOLUNTEER URBAN CONSULTING GROUP. 300 East 42nd Street, New York, N. Y. 10017.

WADSWORTH PUB. CO. 10 Davis Drive, Belmont, Calif. 94002.

WALL STREET REPORTS. 54 Wall Street, New York, N. Y. 10005.

WALLINGFORD GROUP. 4766 Wallingford Street, Pittsburgh, Pa. 15213.

WARNER PAPERBACK LIBRARY. 75 Rockefeller Plaza, New York, N. Y. 10019.

WASHINGTON INTERNATIONAL ARTS LETTER. 325 Pennsylvania Avenue, N. E. , Washington, D. C. 20003.

WATSON-GUPTILL. 2160 Patterson Street, Cincinnati, Ohio 45214.

WESTERN PUB. CO. Department M, 1220 Mound Avenue, Racine, Wis. 53404.

WESTERN STATE ARTS FOUNDATION, INC. 1715 Market Street, Denver, Colo. 80202.

JOHN WILEY. 605 Third Avenue, New York, N. Y. 10016.

WILEY-INTERSCIENCE see JOHN WILEY

H. W. WILSON CO. 950 University Avenue, Bronx, N. Y. 10452.

WORLD COLLECTORS ANNUARY. P. O. Box 19, Zandvoort, Holland.

WORLD PUB. CO. 2080 West 117th Street, Lakewood, Ohio 44111.

WRITER'S DIGEST. 9933 Alliance Road, Cincinnati, Ohio 45242.

PETER H. WYDEN see DAVID McKAY

YORK UNIVERSITY PROGRAMME IN ARTS ADMINISTRATION. 4700 Keele Street, Downsview, Ontario M3J, 1B3, Canada.

AUTHOR/TITLE INDEX

145

162 / Index

Lincoln Center for the Performing Arts 119
Linder, Steffan B. 13
Lindey, Alexander 37, 49
Lippitt, Ronald 7, 15, 78, 92
List of Organizations Filing as Private Foundations 20
Little, Stuart W. 83
The Live Performing Arts: Financial Catastrophe or Economic Catharsis 41, 68
Lloyd, Kenneth 33, 41, 83
Los Angeles Community Arts Alliance 73
Los Angeles County, California County Museum of Art 56
Los Angeles Dance Theatre 69
Low Budget Features 45
Lubar, Robert 100
Lyons, Timothy James 49, 65

The MGM Story: The Complete History of Fifty Roaring Years 12, 47, 64
McClellan, Grant S. 37
McClure, Stewart E. 12
McCoy, Garnett 107
McDarrah, Fred W. 6, 89, 108
McDonald, William Francis 29
McEvoy, Annette 42
McGowan, John J. 6, 38, 50
McIlquham, John 20, 101
McLean, Janice 109
McLuhan, Herbert Marshall 13
McMullen, Roy 13
McWhinney, William 41, 56, 73, 77
Magnan, George A. 88
Maguire, Jacquelyn 42
Mahoney, Margaret 10
The Man from Greek and Roman 64
Management and the Arts: A Selected Bibliography 41
Management of American Foundations: Administration, Policies and Social Role 26

Management Science Applications to Leisure-Time Operations 5
A Management Study of an Art Gallery; Its Structure, Sales and Personnel 58
The Managers', Entertainers', and Agents' Book; How to Plan, Plot, Scheme, Learn, Perform, Avoid Dangers, and Enjoy Your Career in the Entertainment Industry 83
Managing Educational Endowments; Report to the Ford Foundation 17
Managing Nonprofit Organizations 17
Managing Today's Radio Station 48
Mandl, Cynthia K. 56, 69
Manhattan Primitive 63
Mann, Peter H. 69
Manser, Gordon 91
Manual for Museums 56, 107
Margolin, Judith B. 17
Margolis, Gerald A. 35
Mark, Charles C. 13, 98
Marketing Art: A Handbook for Artists and Art Dealers 4, 87, 106
Marketing for Nonprofit Organizations 5
Marketing in Nonprofit Organizations 24
Marks, Peter 65
Marranca, Bonnie 102
Martin, Ralph G. 69
Martinson, Jean Ann 22
Marx, Arthur 49, 65
Marx, Samuel 49, 65
Mason, Lauris 88, 107
Mass Media and Communication 52
The Mass Media and Modern Society 50, 78